THE *Missing* SHOP M

TABLE SAW

{ the tool information you need at your fingertips }

skills institute
press

Distributed By
Fox Chapel Publishing

FOX CHAPEL
PUBLISHING

© 2010 by Skills Institute Press LLC
"Missing Shop Manual" series trademark of Skills Institute Press
Published and distributed in North America by Fox Chapel Publishing Company, Inc.

Table Saw is an original work, first published in 2010.

Portions of text and art previously published by and reproduced under license with Direct Holdings Americas Inc.

ISBN 978-1-56523-471-0

Library of Congress Cataloging-in-Publication Data

Table saw.

    p. cm. -- (The missing shop manual)

Includes index.

ISBN: 978-1-56523-471-0

1. Circular saws. 2. Woodwork.
TT186.T3175 2010
684'.083--dc22

2009038218

To learn more about the other great books from Fox Chapel Publishing,
or to find a retailer near you, call toll-free 800-457-9112
or visit us at *www.FoxChapelPublishing.com*.

Note to Authors: We are always looking for talented authors to write new books
in our area of woodworking, design, and related crafts.
Please send a brief letter describing your idea to Acquisition Editor,
970 Broad Street, East Petersburg, PA 17520.

Printed in China
First printing: February 2010

WHAT YOU WILL LEARN

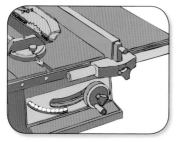

Chapter 1
Choosing a Table Saw, page 6

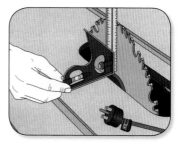

Chapter 2
Table Saw Setup, page 14

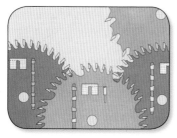

Chapter 3
Table Saw Blades, page 32

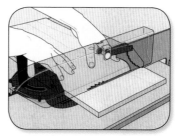

Chapter 4
Table Saw Safety, page 42

Chapter 5
Ripping Wood to Width, page 56

Chapter 6
Crosscutting Wood to Length,
page 70

Chapter 7
Angles and Bevels, page 79

Chapter 8:
Work Supports, page 84

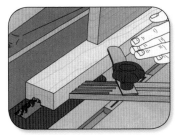

Chapter 9
Dados, Rabbets, and Grooves,
page 98

Chapter 10
Table Saw Joinery, page 106

Chapter 11
Moldings, page 114

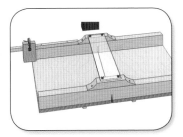

Chapter 12
Table Saw Jigs,
page 122

CHAPTER 1

Choosing a Table Saw

Whether you are working with milled boards from a lumberyard, old barn siding, or sheets of 4-by-8 plywood, the table saw is an excellent all-around tool for cutting wood to width (ripping) and length (crosscutting). The table saw also excels at sawing grooves, at making cuts at an angle (miters) and also with the blade tilted (bevel cuts). If these operations were all it could do it would still be a most valuable tool. But the saw also accepts a variety of blades and accessories, from roller stands that assist with unwieldy panels *(page 62)* to molding heads capable of producing elaborate decorative trim. And with help from the simple, inexpensive shopmade jigs, the table saw is also unsurpassed for repeat cuts and making such fundamental woodworking joints as the lap, box, and open mortise-and-tenon joints *(page 107)*.

The precision and power of a table saw allow for many different cuts with small risk of error. Sawing square and straight with hand tools requires considerable skill and time. Following procedures outlined here can produce clean, accurate cuts consistently with little effort.

With a workpiece clamped firmly to a tenoning jig, cut the tenon part of an open mortise-and-tenon joint.

Table saws are designated according to blade diameter. Models are available in 8-, 10-, and 12-inch sizes. The 8-inch benchtop and 10-inch contractor style models, however, are the most popular home workshop saws. When choosing a table saw, first consider the type of woodworking you will be doing.

The basic requirement for a table saw—for cabinetmaking or general use—is it must be capable of cutting a 2-by-4 at both 90 and 45°. The enclosed stationary saw typically uses a 1.5- to 3-horsepower motor to drive a 10-inch blade. Properly tuned and maintained, it can mill 3-inch stock repeatedly without overheating.

If most of your work is with ¾- or 1-inch-thick stock typically used for cabinetmaking, the open-base contractor's saw is less expensive. It has adequate power and can be mounted on a mobile base.

For occasional use on light stock or where space is at a premium, the 10-inch bench top saw can easily be hauled around the workshop or the job site by one person.

Beware of exaggerated horsepower ratings. Check the motor plate: An honest 1.5-horsepower motor should draw roughly 14 amps at 115 volts; a 3-horsepower motor should draw 14 or 15 amps at 230 volts.

BENCH TOP SAW

With its built-in guides, the table saw sets up quickly for both square and angled cuts. Furthermore, it cuts much more accurately than the hand-held circular saw. Available in full-size and tabletop models, a typical table saw uses 10-inch blades that cut 3½ inches deep. Because table-saw blades cut on the downstroke, cut plywood with the good side up.

A metal rip fence, adjustable along guide bars, ensures a straight cut. There is also a pivoting miter gauge, which slides along a slot in the table, that feeds boards into the blade at any angle. Two controls, the blade-tilt knob and blade-height crank, adjust the angle and height of the blade itself. A table insert, which keeps sawdust from falling into the motor, is removable for changing blades. For safety, a plastic guard covers the blade.

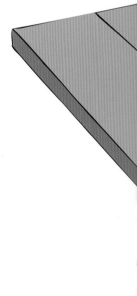

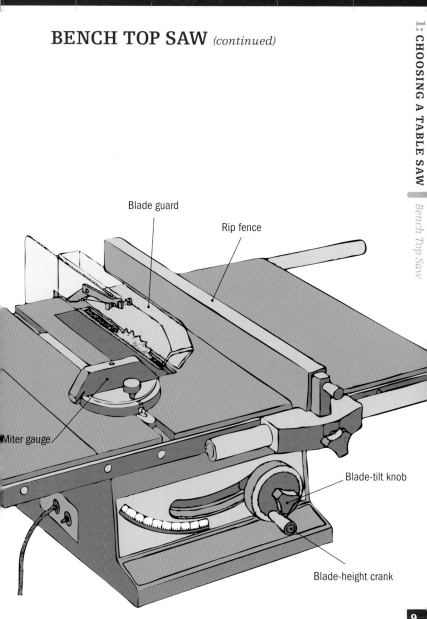

Blade guard

Rip fence

Miter gauge

Blade-tilt knob

Blade-height crank

CONTRACTOR'S SAW

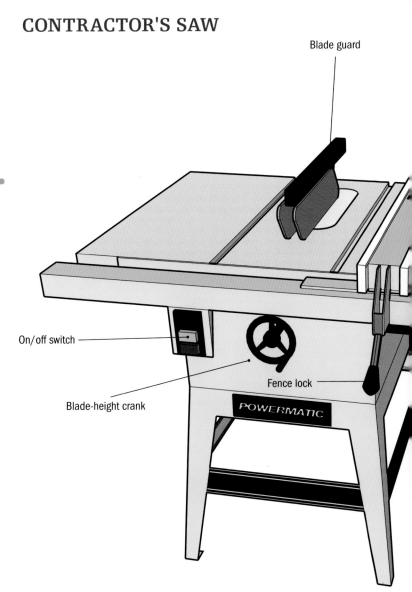

Blade guard

On/off switch

Blade-height crank

Fence lock

POWERMATIC

CONTRACTOR'S SAW *(continued)*

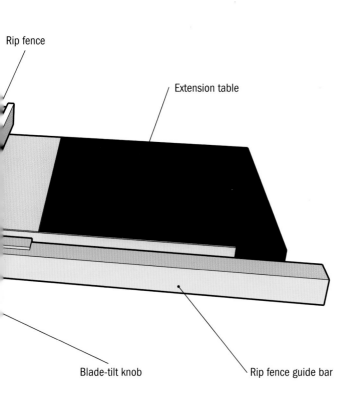

Rip fence

Extension table

Blade-tilt knob

Rip fence guide bar

CABINET SAW

Blade guard
Clear shield that protects operator from blade bolted to splitter and anti-kickback device

Auxiliary table inserts
Keep wood pieces from falling into table; wider slots for dado or molding head

Standard table insert
Keeps wood pieces from falling into table

Miter gauge
Guides workpiece across table for crosscutting; wooden extension can be screwed to gauge to support wide panels

Roller stand
Supports long workpieces during cutting operations

Rip fence
Guides workpiece across table for ripping

On/off switch
Magnetic switch turns off saw if machine is unplugged

Blade angle scale

Blade height adjustment crank

Blade height adjustment crank

Lock knob
Holds crank at fixed setting; tightened firmly before saw is operated

Vacuum attachment
For dust collection system

Mobile base
Facilitates moving the saw aside in small shops; wheels can be locked in position

CABINET SAW *(continued)*

Hold-down device
Holds workpiece firmly against both table and rip fence for safe rip cuts

Optional rip fence
Longer fence replaces standard fence when extension table used

Auxiliary fence
Board clamped or screwed to rip fence extends height of fence and protects it

Extension table
Increases work surface to facilitate cutting large boards and panels

Rip fence guide bar
Holds optional rip fence to extension table; features rule for measuring width of cut

Fence lock
Holds rip fence in fixed position

CHAPTER 2

Table Saw Setup

Whether your table saw sits poised to make its first cut, or is a seasoned machine with a home full of furniture to its credit, it cannot cut with precision unless its adjustable parts are in proper alignment. A table saw with misaligned parts can result in any one of several frustrating problems, including excessive vibration, increased risk of kickback, blade damage, burn marks on workpieces, and inaccurate cuts. Even errors as little as 1/64 inch can compromise the quality and strength of a piece of furniture. The normal forces of routine use will eventually throw a table saw out of alignment. Even a new machine straight off the assembly line usually needs a certain amount of adjustment before it can perform safely and properly.

The table saw components that need to be checked and aligned are those that come in contact with the workpiece during the cut: the blade, table, miter gauge, rip fence, and splitter or riving knife. If any of these parts is not in proper alignment, you risk burn marks, tapered cuts, or kickback.

The simple tune-up procedures shown on the pages that follow will improve the performance of any table saw. It is a good idea to take the time to undertake them before starting a new project. For the sake of efficiency, follow the steps in the order they appear. You will only be able to align the miter gauge with the saw blade, for example, if the table has been squared with the blade. For safety, remember to unplug your saw before performing these checks and adjustments.

To confirm that your table saw is properly tuned, make a few test cuts. A good way to ensure your saw is cutting in precise, straight lines is to cut a squared board in two and flip one of the pieces over. Butt the two cut ends together. They should fit together without any gaps as perfectly as they did before the board was flipped, as shown on page 21.

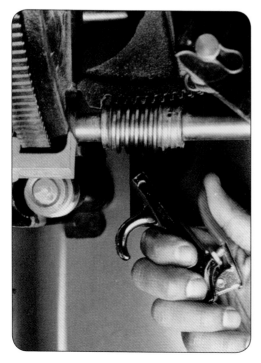

Most table saws feature worm gear and rack mechanisms connected to crank wheels to raise and tilt the arbor assembly and blade. These mechanisms can become caked with pitch and sawdust, preventing the saw from operating smoothly. In the photo at left, compressed air is being used to clean the blade height mechanism.

CHECKING TABLE ALIGNMENT

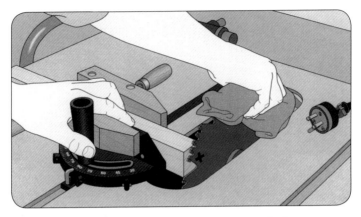

The face of the miter gauge and the blade must be perfectly
perpendicular. To check this, position the miter gauge at the front of the
saw blade. Clamp a square wood block against the miter gauge with the
end of the block butted against a saw blade tooth. Mark an X on the
blade next to the tooth; this will enable you to check the same section
of blade should you need to repeat the test. Slide the miter gauge and
the block together toward the back of the table while rotating the blade
by hand *(above)*. The block should remain butted against the tooth as
the blade rotates from front to back. If a gap opens between the block
and the tooth, or the block binds against the blade as it is rotated, you
will need to align the table. Be certain to unplug the saw before you
work on it.

ALIGNING THE TABLE

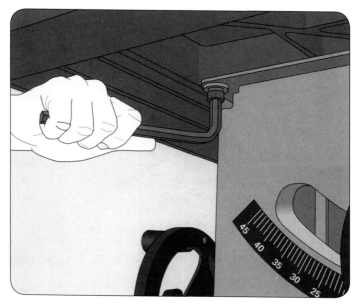

Adjust the saw table following the owner's manual instructions. For the model shown, use a hex wrench to loosen the table bolts that secure the top to the saw stand *(above)*; the bolts are located under the table. Loosen all but one of the bolts and adjust the table position slightly; the bolt you leave tightened will act as a pivot, simplifying the alignment process. Repeat the blade test. Once the table is correctly aligned with the blade, tighten the table bolts.

Unplug the saw and remove the table insert, then butt a combination square against the saw blade between two teeth *(above)*. The blade of the square should fit flush against the saw blade. If there is a gap between the two, rotate the blade angle adjustment crank until the saw blade rests flush against the square's blade. Reposition the angle adjustment stop so that the blade will return to its proper position each time it is adjusted.

SQUARING MITER GAUGE

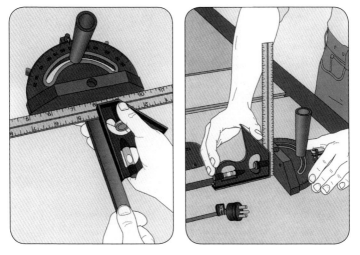

With the miter gauge out of the table slot, use a combination square to confirm the face of the gauge is square with the edge of the gauge bar *(above, left)*. If it is not, use the adjustment handle on the gauge to square the two. Then place the miter gauge in its table slot and butt the square against the gauge *(above, right)*. The blade of the square should fit flush against the gauge. If there is a gap between the two, have the gauge machined square at a metal-working shop.

ALIGNING MITER GAUGE

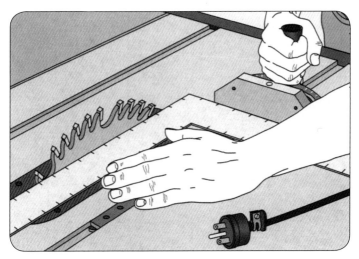

Butt a carpenter's square against the miter gauge and the saw blade between two teeth. The square should fit flush against the gauge. If there is a gap between the two, loosen the adjustment handle on the gauge *(above)* and swivel the miter head to bring it flush against the square. Tighten the adjustment handle on the gauge.

*Shop*Tip

To eliminate excessive side-to-side play of the miter gauge, remove the gauge and place the bar edge up on a board. Use a ball-peen hammer and a prick punch to strike the edge of the bar in a staggered pattern every inch along it. This will raise bumps on the edge of the bar for a tighter fit in the slot. If is too tight, file bumps down.

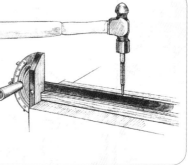

CHECKING SAW ALIGNMENT

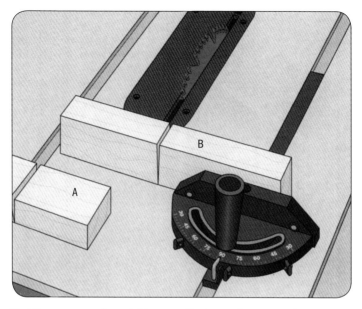

Test the accuracy of your table saw adjustments by crosscutting a couple of scrap boards. To check the blade-to-table alignment, mark an X on a board and cut it face down at your mark. Then turn the cutoff over and hold the cut ends together *(board A in the illustration)*. Any gap between the two ends represents twice the error in the table alignment; if necessary, repeat the test shown on page 20. To check the miter gauge adjustment, crosscut the second board, face down as well, flip one piece over, and butt the two pieces together on edge *(board B)*. Again, any gap represents twice the error in the adjustment. If necessary, square the miter gauge again *(page 20)*.

ALIGNING RIP FENCE

Lock the rip fence in place alongside the miter slot. If the fence and the slot are not parallel, adjust the angle of the fence following the manufacturer's instructions. Some models feature adjustment bolts at the front of the table that you can loosen or tighten with a hex wrench to change the alignment *(right, above);* others have fence adjustment bolts that you can loosen with a wrench *(right, below).* For this model, adjust the fence parallel to the miter slot, then retighten the adjustment bolts.

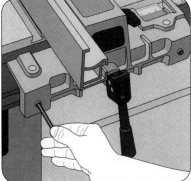

LEVELING TABLE INSERT

To set the table insert level with the saw table, place a square board across the insert and the table. Adjust the leveling screws at the corners of the insert with a hex wrench *(right)* until the insert is flush with the tabletop. You can also adjust the insert slightly below the table at the front and slightly above the table at the back; this will prevent the workpiece from catching or binding on the insert during the cut. If your saw's insert does not have leveling screws, file or shim the insert to make it lie flush with the table.

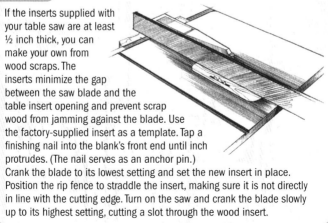

*Shop*Tip

If the inserts supplied with your table saw are at least ½ inch thick, you can make your own from wood scraps. The inserts minimize the gap between the saw blade and the table insert opening and prevent scrap wood from jamming against the blade. Use the factory-supplied insert as a template. Tap a finishing nail into the blank's front end until inch protrudes. (The nail serves as an anchor pin.) Crank the blade to its lowest setting and set the new insert in place. Position the rip fence to straddle the insert, making sure it is not directly in line with the cutting edge. Turn on the saw and crank the blade slowly up to its highest setting, cutting a slot through the wood insert.

ADJUSTING HEIGHT AND TILT MECHANISMS

If your table saw's blade sticks or moves sluggishly when you raise or tilt it, clean the height and tilt adjustment mechanisms. Start by removing the tabletop following the manufacturer's instructions. Blow out the sawdust with compressed air, then clean the moving parts. Start with the blade height and tilt mechanisms (right), using solvent and a brass-bristle brush to remove pitch and hardened sawdust deposits. Scrub the machined ways on the front and rear trunnions (above, top). Once all the parts are clean, lubricate all the moving parts with a graphite or silicon-based lubricant. Replace the tabletop and fine-tune the saw (page 18).

SETTING BLADE HEIGHT

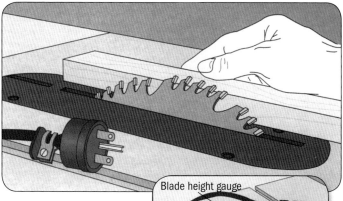

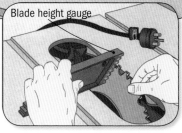

Blade height gauge

A blade that is too high poses a safety risk; one that is too low will not cut properly. For most cutting operations, unplug the saw and rotate the blade height adjustment crank until about ¼ inch of the blade is visible above the workpiece *(above, top)*. To set the blade at a specific height, use a tape measure or a commercially made gauge, which features a series of steps of ¼-inch increments; a similar gauge can be shop-built from scraps of ¼-inch plywood (next page). The blade is at the correct height when it rubs the gauge at the desired height as you rotate the blade by hand *(inset)*.

BLADE HEIGHT GAUGE

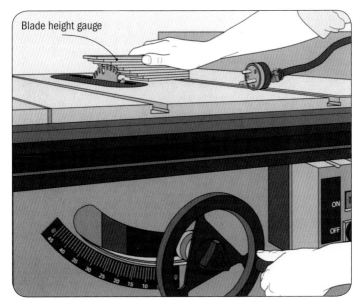

Blade height gauge

Your table saw's blade can be set at a specific height quickly with a blade height gauge. Make the jig from strips of ⅛- or ¹⁄₁₆-inch-thick hardboard or solid wood laminated together. First, rip a length of the stock to a width of 3 inches. Crosscut the piece into strips, starting with an 8-inch length. Make each successive strip ⅜ inch shorter than the previous one. Once all the strips are cut, glue them together face-to-face with one end aligned. To use the jig, set it on the saw table beside the blade and rotate the blade height adjustment crank until the blade contacts the gauge at the desired height *(above)*.

SETTING BLADE ANGLE

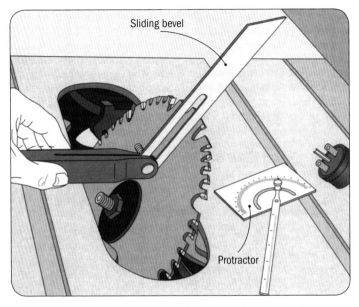

Sliding bevel

Protractor

To make an angle cut, remove the table insert and crank the blade to its highest setting. Use a protractor to set the desired cutting angle on a sliding bevel and butt the bevel against the blade between two teeth. Rotate the angle adjustment crank on the saw until the blade rests flush against the bevel *(above)*.

DRIVE BELTS

Too much belt tension can strain a stationary tool's motor bearings, while too little tension often leads to slippage and excessive wear. To check drive belt tension, unplug the tool and remove the panel covering the belt. Then pinch the belt between the pulleys with one hand *(top)*.

The amount of deflection will vary with the tool; as a rule of thumb, the belt should flex $\frac{1}{32}$ inch for every inch of span between pulleys. If there is too little or too much tension, adjust it following the manufacturer's instructions. Any drive belt that is cracked or worn should be replaced. For smooth operation, the pulleys should be aligned; if they are not, loosen the adjustment setscrew on the motor pulley with a hex wrench *(bottom)*, and slide the pulley in line with the other pulley.

Pulley adjustment setscrew

MAINTAINING TABLETOPS

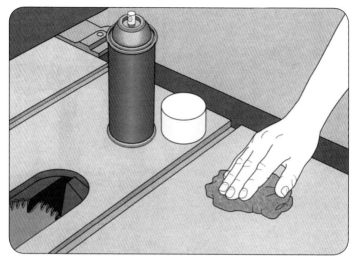

Cleaning Stationary Machine Tabletops

To keep stock running smoothly, clean the tabletop frequently, wiping off any pitch or gum deposits with a rag and mineral spirits. Remove any rust or pitting with fine steel wool and penetrating oil (above), then wipe off any residue and sand the area with fine sandpaper. A coat of paste wax rubbed on and then buffed will make pushing wood into the cutting edge much less tiring.

MAINTAINING SWITCHES

The switches on stationary tools can become clogged, causing the switch to stick or even preventing it from operating. If the switch sticks, unplug the tool, remove the switch cover and clean the switch immediately. To prevent such problems, periodically clean out the switch by blowing compressed air into it *(above)*.

RIVING KNIFE, ANTIKICKBACK FINGERS

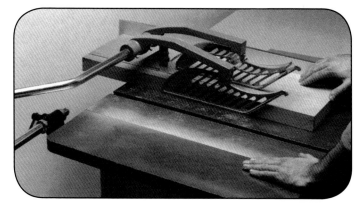

The riving knife or splitter can be knocked out of alignment with the saw blade. With the saw unplugged, lift the guard and set a straight edge across the plate of the saw blade and the face of the riving knife. Adjust the mounting bolts and washers until the riving knife lines up with the saw blade on both sides.

Make sure the blade guard moves smoothly up and down, without binding. Clean any pitch or debris from the guard apparatus. File the anti-kickback fingers so they are sharp and without burrs. The anti-kickback fingers should be sharp enough to dig into a piece of wood and stop it, in the event of a kickback.

On older saws, the riving knife mounts to a fixed bolt underneath the saw table. Consequently it does not rise and fall with the saw blade, and it must be removed for grooving cuts. On newer saws, the riving knife is mounted on the blade elevation apparatus, so that it does rise and fall along with the saw blade. A riving knife that rises and falls does not need to be removed for grooving cuts. It is much safer than the old style of knife.

CHAPTER 3

Table Saw Blades

A table saw is only as good as the saw blade it turns. A dull or chipped blade can transform even the best of table saws into a poor or dangerous tool. To protect blades from damage, avoid stacking them directly atop each other. Hang them individually on hooks or place cardboard between them. Replace a blade that is dull or cracked or has chipped teeth; more accidents are caused by dull blades than sharp ones.

Keep your saw blades clean. Wood resins can gum up a blade and hamper its ability to make a smooth cut. To clean sticky wood resin and pitch off a blade, soak it in turpentine, then scrub it with steel wool. Spray-on oven cleaner can be used to dissolve stubborn deposits.

Proper blade performance is as much a matter of using the right blade for the job as keeping it clean and in good condition. As illustrated, there are blades designed specifically for crosscutting or ripping, others to minimize kickback or produce thin kerfs, and blades for cutting specific types of wood. Regardless of type, all blades are installed on the saw and adjusted for cutting height and angle in the same way *(pages 22–23)*.

The most important advance in recent years has been the introduction of carbide-tipped blades. These have eclipsed traditional high-speed

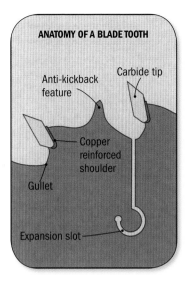

ANATOMY OF A BLADE TOOTH

Anti-kickback feature

Carbide tip

Copper reinforced shoulder

Gullet

Expansion slot

steel as the blade of choice. The advantage of carbide-tipped blades lies in their ability to keep a sharp edge far longer than their steel counterparts. Composed of grains of hard tungsten-carbon particles one-hundredth the thickness of a human hair, the carbide chunks are bonded with cobalt and brazed onto the blade with copper or silver. Carbide is extremely hard; the highest rating—C4—has a hardness value of 94 on a scale that rates diamond as 100.

While carbide-tipped blades can stay sharp for a hundred hours or more of use, they are more difficult—and therefore more expensive—to sharpen than high-speed steel blades. Still, most woodworkers believe the price is worth paying for the advantages they offer.

In any event, before you send a carbide blade out for resharpening, clean it thoroughly to remove all pitch and gum deposits. In most cases, that's enough—the clean blade will perform as if it was new.

CARBIDE BLADES

Brazed to a shoulder on the saw blade, the carbide tip does the cutting, while the gullet removes the sawdust. The expansion slot prevents the blade from warping when it heats up. The anti-kickback feature reduces the risk that the blade will jam, and send a workpiece flying back toward the user.

Carbide-tipped saw blades feature four basic tooth designs. Each has its own advantages and applications. All blades have teeth that shear through wood and gullets that clear away sawdust and wood chips from the kerf. Some blades have rakers that cut out material left in the kerf by the teeth. On some blades, the teeth are alternately beveled—they shear stock alternately from one side, and then the other side of the cut.

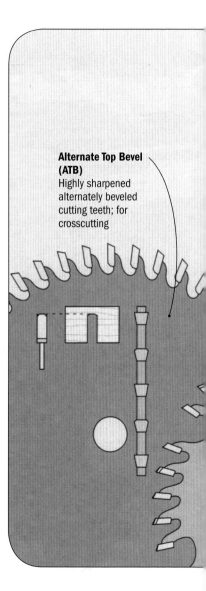

Alternate Top Bevel (ATB)
Highly sharpened alternately beveled cutting teeth; for crosscutting

Triple Chip Grind (TCG)

Cutting teeth with edges ground to 45° alternate with flat-top raker teeth; for ripping or crosscutting abrasive materials

Alternate Top Bevel with a Raker (ATB/R)

Four alternately beveled cutting teeth alternate with a flat-top raker tooth; for ripping or crosscutting.

Flat Top Grind (FTG)

Flat-top cutting teeth; for ripping

BLADE TYPES

Rip Blade
(Standard)
For cuts along the grain. Has deep gullets and relatively few, large teeth. The chisel-like cutting edges of the teeth make a fairly rough cut and produce large particles of sawdust and wood chips.

Crosscut Blade
(Standard)
For cuts across the grain. Has more teeth than rip blade. The teeth make a smooth cut and produce fine sawdust.

Crosscut Blade
(Anti-kickback)
A variation of the standard crosscut blade. The projection between the teeth limits the size of the chips made with each bite; less aggressive bites prevent kickback.

Combination Blade
A general-purpose blade for ripping or crosscutting; does not make as smooth a cut as a rip or crosscut blade, but makes frequent blade changes unnecessary.

BLADE TYPES *(continued)*

Hollow Ground Planer Blade
(High-Speed Steel)
For very smooth crosscuts, rip cuts or angle cuts. The body of the blade is thinner than the hub and teeth, which are not set, ensuring that the body does not bind in the saw kerf.

Melamine Blade
Has many small teeth designed to cut through the abrasive glue found in particleboard and other manufactured panels, resulting in a chip-free cut.

Crosscut Blade
(Thin Rim)
A variation of the standard crosscut blade for fine finish cuts, its thinner rim produces a narrower kerf, putting less strain on the saw motor.

Plywood Blade
(High-Speed Steel)
Has many small teeth that made a smooth, splinter-free cut in plywood and wood veneers. The teeth are less efficient in highly abrasive manufactured panels such as particleboard.

CHANGING A BLADE

Removing Old Blade

Always unplug the saw before working on the blade. Working at the front of the table, wedge a piece of scrap wood under a blade tooth to prevent the blade from turning. Use the wrench supplied with the saw to loosen the arbor nut *(above).* (Table saw arbors usually have reverse threads; the nut is loosened in a clockwise direction—not counterclockwise.) Finish loosening the nut by hand, making sure that it does not fall into the machine. Carefully lift the blade and washer off the arbor.

CHANGING A BLADE *(continued)*

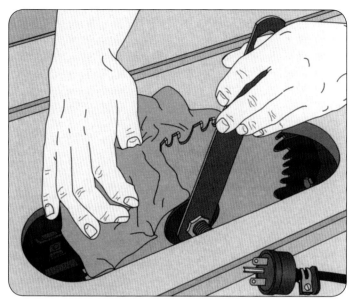

Installing New Blade

Slide the blade on the arbor with its teeth pointing in the direction of blade rotation (toward the front of the table). Insert the washer and nut and start tightening by hand. To finish tightening, grip the saw blade with a rag and use the wrench supplied with the saw *(above)*. Do not use a piece of wood as a wedge as this could result in overtightening the nut.

CLEANING SAW BLADES

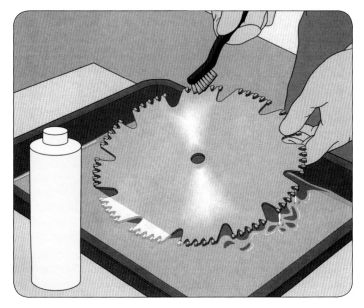

Clean the blade using a commercial resin solvent. (Commercial oven cleaner, turpentine, or a solution of hot water with ammonia may also be used.) For stubborn pitch and gum deposits, soak the blade in the cleaning agent in a shallow pan and use a brass-bristled brush to clean the teeth *(above)*.

BLADE STORAGE

Storage Box

Organize your circular saw blades in a custom-made storage box like the one shown at right. Build the box from ¾-inch plywood, cutting it a few inches larger than your largest blade and wide enough to hold all your blades. Make the bottom and back

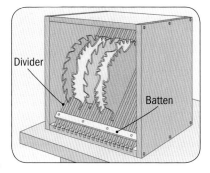

Divider

Batten

from the same piece, routing the dadoes for the dividers first and then cutting the piece in two. This will ensure perfect alignment of the dadoes. Cut the dadoes ¼ inch deep and wide, spaced at ½-inch intervals. Make the dividers out of ¼-inch plywood or hardboard. Fit the dividers in their dadoes, glue them to the bottom and back, then screw the box together. To keep the blades from rolling out of the box, cut a batten from scrap stock and nail it to the dividers near the bottom of the box.

Blade Carrier

The commercial blade carrier shown at right is a handy storage device that will protect your circular saw blades from damage and make it easier to transport them. This model accommodates up to ten 10-inch blades.

Table Saw Safety

Safety is as much a matter of attitude and common sense as correct technique.

The table saw is a powerful machine; all of the safety devices in the world will not make up for a cavalier attitude or sloppy work practices. On the other hand, a woodworker should not approach a table saw with trepidation; a timid operator, someone reluctant to hold a workpiece firmly while cutting it, faces as many risks as a careless worker. Caution mixed with confidence stemming from an understanding of the machine and the task at hand should be the woodworker's guide.

Read the owner's manual supplied with your saw. Before starting a job, make sure you know how to use the safety accessories that are designed to protect you from specific injuries while operating the machine. Use devices like push sticks and featherboards, as shown throughout this chapter, to protect your fingers from the blade. A hold-down device, is also a worthwhile investment. And remember that not only your fingers and hands are at risk: A safe workshop also includes hearing protectors, safety glasses, and dust masks.

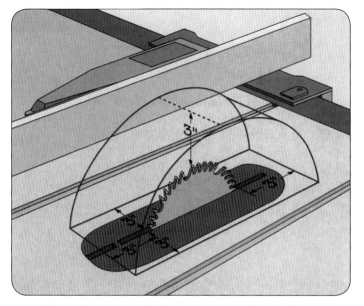

To avoid injury from the saw blade, constantly be alert to a "danger zone" that exists within about 3 inches of the blade—both above and to either side of it (above). Keep your hands out of this zone whenever the saw is being used—even if the blade guard is in place. To feed a workpiece past the blade within the zone, use a push stick, a push block, or a jig.

SAFETY TIPS

- Use a safety guard whenever possible. Before making a bevel cut, confirm that the guard will be clear of the blade.

- Always unplug a saw before working on it.

- Do not leave the saw running when it is unattended.

- If you are interrupted, complete the operation under way before turning off the saw and looking up.

- Follow the manufacturer's instructions to change accessories; unplug the saw first. Make sure that saw blades and cutters are sharp, clean, and undamaged.

- Before cutting a workpiece, remove any loose knots from it using a hammer. Inspect salvaged wood for nails and screws before cutting.

- Do not start a cut until the blade is running at full speed.

- Before using the saw each time, inspect its safety features. Make sure there is no binding or misalignment of moving parts. Do not use the saw until such problems are corrected.

- Always feed wood into the saw blade against the direction of blade rotation.

SAFETY TIPS *(continued)*

- Make sure the rip fence is locked in position before ripping.

- Do not use the miter gauge in combination with the rip fence to make a cut—except when the blade does not cut completely through the workpiece, such as for a dado or a groove.

- Use the rip fence or the miter gauge for all cutting operations; never attempt to cut freehand.

- Before ripping a board, ensure the edge in contact with the rip fence is smooth and straight and the surface against the table is flat.

- Stand to one side of any workpiece during any cutting operation in case of kickback.

- If you have to reach past the blade, keep your hands at least 3 inches away from it.

- Use a wooden stick, rather than your fingers, to clear wood scraps from the saw table.

BLADE GUARD AND SPLITTER

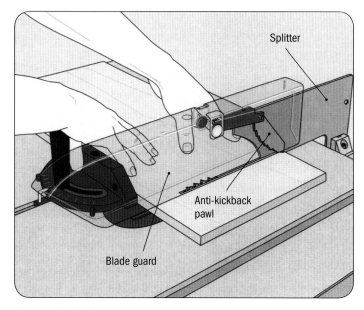

Splitter

Anti-kickback
pawl

Blade guard

The standard table saw blade guard assembly includes a pivoting, clear-plastic blade guard, which deflects flying wood chips and reduces the chance that fingers will slip accidentally into the blade. The guard is connected to a thin piece of metal known as the splitter or riving knife. Attached directly in line with the blade, the splitter keeps the saw cut—or kerf—open. Without such a device, the kerf may close during a cut, binding the blade and throwing the workpiece back toward the operator with great force. Kickback can also result if a workpiece jams between the blade and the rip fence. Further protection from kickback is provided by a metal finger (or fingers) called an anti-kickback pawl, which normally rides on the surface of the workpiece. In the event of kickback, the finger digs in, preventing the workpiece from flying back.

BLADE GUARD AND SPLITTER *(continued)*

Optional guards like the one shown at right provide extra flexibility. Held in place by a cantilevered arm bolted to the side of the saw table, it features a plastic shield raised and lowered by a crank. Resting lightly on

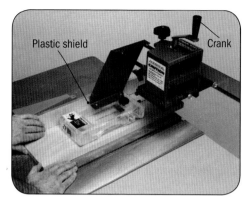

Plastic shield

Crank

the workpiece, the shield serves as a hold-down and provides wide coverage of the cutting area, allowing the woodworker to perform operations such as cove cutting and rabbeting, which cannot be done with conventional guards in position. The blade guard shown above has two arms. For most cuts, both arms ride on top of the workpiece, but when the blade is close to the rip fence one of the arms can be raised out of the way. The guard can also be used without the retractable splitter when cutting dadoes and grooves.

PUSH STICKS

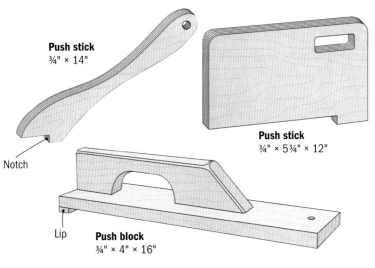

Push stick
¾" × 14"

Push stick
¾" × 5¾" × 12"

Notch

Lip

Push block
¾" × 4" × 16"

Push sticks and push blocks for feeding stock across the table of a
stationary power tool can be made using ¾-inch plywood or solid
stock. No one shape is ideal; a well-designed push stick should be
comfortable to use and suitable for the machine and task at hand.
For most cuts on a table saw, design a push stick with a 45° angle
between the handle and the base (top, left). The notch on the bottom
edge must be deep enough to support the workpiece, but shallow
enough not to contact the saw table. The long base of a rectangular
push stick (top, right) enables you to apply downward pressure on a
workpiece. For surfacing the face of a board on a jointer, the long, wide
base of a push block (above, bottom) is ideal. It features a lip glued to
the underside of the base, flush with one end. Screw the handle to the
top, positioning it so the back is even with the end of the base.

FEATHERBOARDS

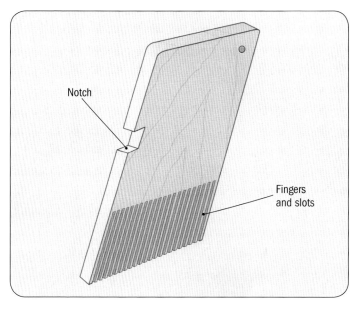

Notch

Fingers and slots

Featherboards serve as anti-kickback devices, because the fingers allow the workpiece to move in only one direction—toward a stationary tool's bit or blade. To make a featherboard like the one shown above, cut a 30° to 45° miter at one end of a ¾-inch-thick, 3- to 4-inch-wide board; the length of the jig can be varied to suit the work you plan to do. Mark a parallel line about 5 inches from the mitered end and cut a series of slots to the marked line on the band saw, spacing the kerfs about ⅛ inch apart to create a row of sturdy but pliable fingers. Finally, cut a notch out of one edge of the featherboard to accommodate a support board.

USING PUSH STICKS

Push sticks and featherboards make an operation like ripping on the table saw much safer by keeping your hands well away from the blade. The push stick is used to feed the stock and keep it flat on the table, while the featherboard presses the workpiece against the fence. The featherboard shown in the photo is secured to the table with special hardware rather than with clamps. A clamping bar in the miter slot features two screws that can be tightened, causing the bar to expand and lock tightly in the slot.

USING FEATHERBOARDS

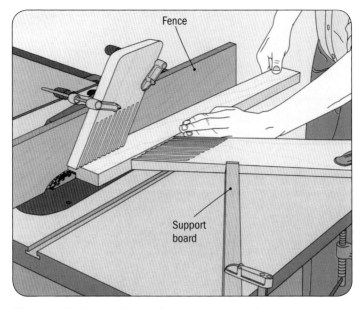

Fence

Support
board

Clamp one featherboard to the fence above the blade, and place a
longer one halfway between the blade and the front of the table. Clamp
a support board in the notch perpendicular to the horizontal featherboard to prevent it from creeping out of place during the cut. For the
operation shown above, feed the workpiece into the blade until your
trailing fingers reach the featherboards. Then use a push stick to finish
the cut, or move to the back of the table with the saw still running and
pull the workpiece past the blade.

BEVELED FEATHERBOARD

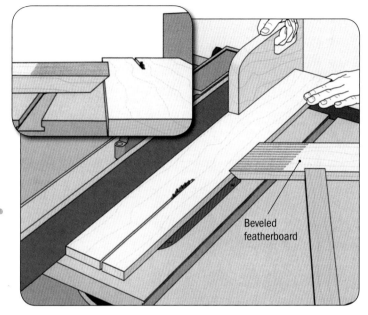

Beveled
featherboard

A featherboard clamped to the fence of a table saw, as shown on the previous page, can get in the way of a push stick during a rip cut. A featherboard with a beveled end will press a workpiece against both the fence and saw table, eliminating the need to clamp a featherboard to the fence (above). Make the device as you would a standard featherboard (page 49), but cut a 45° bevel on its leading end before cutting the fingers and slots. Also make sure that the featherboard is thicker than the stock you are ripping (inset).

SHIMMED FEATHERBOARD

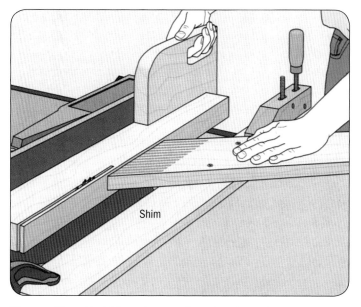

Shim

When working with thick stock or running a board on edge across a saw table, a featherboard clamped directly to the table may apply pressure too low on the workpiece, causing it to tilt away from the fence. To apply pressure closer to the middle of the stock, screw the featherboard to a shim and then clamp the shim to the table (above).

VACUUM SYSTEM

The heart of the vacuum system is the pump, here a ⅓ horsepower oil-less model, which draws air at a maximum of 4.5 cubic feet per minute. The hose features a quick coupler that attaches to a connector that is screwed into a hole through the template or featherboard. You will also need to use vacuum tape or closed-cell foam weatherstripping as a gasket to seal the cavity between template and workpiece or featherboard and work table.

The vacuum system shown here is an excellent way to anchor featherboards to work tables and fasten templates to workpieces. The system is more convenient than conventional clamping and offers as much holding power with out risking damage to stock. The only limitation is that mating surfaces must be flat and smooth.

To set up a vacuum system, you need the parts shown in the photo below. The tape is fastened to the underside of the featherboard or template, creating a cavity. The hose from the pump is inserted in a hole in the featherboard or template. When the jig is placed on the surface, the pump sucks the air from the cavity, producing a vacuum. Any pump rated at 3 cubic feet per minute or higher is adequate for the home workshop. If you own a compressor, you can convert it into a vacuum pump with a transducing pump.

VACUUM FEATHERBOARD

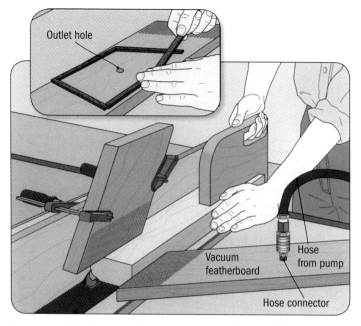

Outlet hole

Vacuum featherboard

Hose from pump

Hose connector

Bore an outlet hole through the center of the featherboard. The hole's diameter should be slightly less than that of the threaded end of the hose connector you will use. Next, apply four strips of closed-cell vacuum tape to the underside of the featherboard, forming a quadrilateral with no gaps (inset). Screw the hose connector into the outlet hole on the top face of the featherboard; use a wrench. To set up the vacuum jig, place the featherboard on the saw table—for the molding cut shown, it is positioned to press the workpiece against the fence. Make certain the tape strips are flat on the table. Snap the quick coupler at the end of the vacuum pump hose onto the hose connector and turn on the pump. Air pressure will anchor the featherboard to the table as you feed the workpiece through the cut (above).

CHAPTER 5:
Ripping Wood to Width

Ripping has traditionally been defined as "cutting with the grain." But some woods today—plywood and particleboard, for example—have no overall grain. A more appropriate description focuses on the table saw accessory used to make a rip cut. Whereas crosscutting is done using the miter gauge, ripping involves the rip fence. (Except for certain cuts that do not pass completely through the workpiece, such as a dado cut, the rip fence and miter gauge should never be used at the same time, or jamming and kickback can occur.)

Before ripping a workpiece, set the height of the saw blade, then lock the rip fence in position for the cut width. Keep your hands out of the blade's path. For protection, use accessories such as push sticks, featherboards and hold-down devices.

To use a hold-down device, it may first be necessary to screw a wood auxiliary fence to the rip fence. Auxiliary fences are ideal surfaces for clamping; many woodworkers make them a permanent fixture on their saws.

STARTING THE CUT

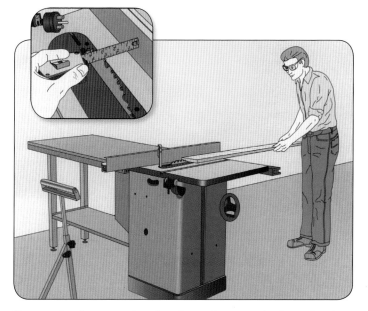

Measure the distance to the edge of a tooth nearest the fence (inset). Position the fence and set one end of the workpiece on the saw table close to the blade. Use your left hand to press the wood down on the table and flush with the fence; use your right hand to feed the wood into the blade (above). Continue feeding the board into the blade at a steady rate until the trailing end of the board approaches the table. **(Caution: Blade guard removed for clarity.)**

APPROACHING THE BLADE

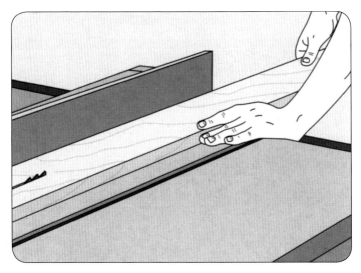

Hook the thumb of your left hand over the edge of the table and rest your palm on the table, keeping the wood pressed down firmly on the table and up against the fence (above). Continue feeding the board with your right hand until the trailing end of the board approaches the blade.

PASSING THE BLADE

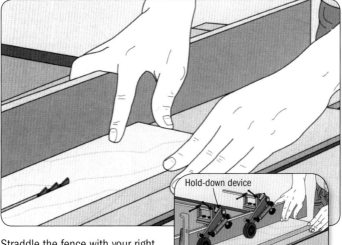

Hold-down device

Riving Knife with antikick back fingers

Straddle the fence with your right hand (above), making sure neither hand is in line with the blade. If any finger comes within 3 inches of the blade, complete the cut using a push stick, or a jig. In the inset drawing, the wheels of the hold-down device keep the workpiece firmly against the table; to prevent kickback, they also lock when pushed against the direction of the cut, keeping the board from shooting backward. If using a hold-down device, begin feeding the workpiece from the front of the table, then move to the back to pull the wood through. Otherwise, finish the cut from the front of the table.

COMPLETING THE CUT

Keep pushing the board until the blade cuts through it completely.
When the workpiece is clear of the blade, use your left hand to shift the
waste piece to the left side of the table *(above)*. With your right hand,
carefully lift the good piece and place it to the right of the rip fence
before turning off the saw. Do not allow pieces of wood to pile up on
the saw table.

Hands-Free Off Switch

To turn off the saw when your hands are busy on the table, use a shop made knee or foot lever. Cut a board equal in width to the switch box. The board should be long enough to reach with a foot or a knee when attached to the box (right). Screw a hinge to one end of the board and position the hinge on top of the box. Mark the spot where the ON button touches the board. Cut a hole through the board at this mark. Attach the hinge to the box using glue, or remove the cover and drive in screws.

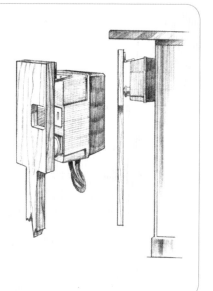

RIPPING A LARGE PANEL

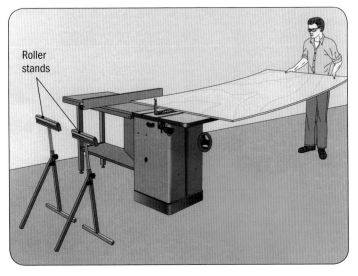

Roller stands

Starting the Cut

Position the rip fence for the width of cut. Ask someone to stand at the back of the table to receive the cut sections; otherwise, set up two roller stands. Position them so that, depending on the thickness of the panel, they are close enough to support the cut pieces. Lay the panel on the saw table a few inches from the blade, butting its edge against the fence. To begin the cut, slowly feed the panel into the blade, slightly raising the panel's back end to keep its front end flat; apply enough side pressure with your left hand to keep the panel butted squarely against the fence *(above)*. Continue feeding the panel into the blade at a steady rate until its back end reaches the edge of the table.

(Caution: Blade guard removed for clarity.)

RIPPING A LARGE PANEL *(continued)*

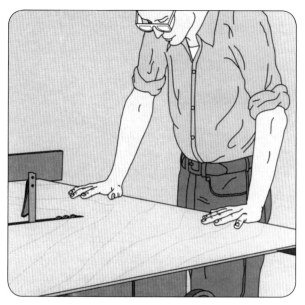

Completing the Cut

Standing to the left of the saw blade, position your palms on the back end of the panel so that neither hand is in line with the blade. Press down on the panel with your palms *(above)* and push the trailing end of the panel toward the blade until the cut is completed.

RIPPING NARROW STRIPS

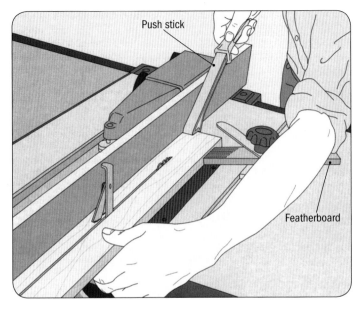

Push stick

Featherboard

Position the rip fence for the width of cut. Then butt the workpiece against the fence. To keep your hands away from the blade as it cuts the workpiece, use two accessories—a featherboard and a push stick. Clamp a featherboard to the saw table—the model shown is installed in the miter slot—so that its fingers hold the workpiece snugly against the fence. Use a push stick as shown to feed the workpiece into the blade. Continue cutting steadily until the blade nears the end of the cut. Support the waste piece with your left hand; to prevent your hand from being pulled back into the blade in case of kickback, curl your fingers around the edge of the table *(above).* **(Caution: Blade guard removed for clarity.)**

JIG FOR REPEAT RIPS

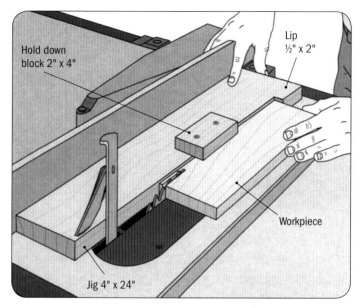

Hold down
block 2" x 4"

Lip
½" x 2"

Workpiece

Jig 4" x 24"

To rip several narrow strips to the same width, use the shopmade jig
shown above. For the jig, cut a board with a lip at one end. Screw
a hold-down block to the jig, then butt the jig flush against the rip
fence. Mark a cutting line on the workpiece, then seat it against the jig,
flush with the lip. Position the rip fence so that the cutting line on the
workpiece is aligned with the saw blade.

   To make each cut, slide the jig and the workpiece as a unit across
the table, feeding the workpiece into the blade *(above)*. (The first cut
will trim the lip to the width of the cut.) Use your left hand to keep the
workpiece flush against the jig. Remove the cut strip, reposition the
workpiece in the jig, and repeat for identical strips. **(Caution: Blade
guard removed for clarity.)**

RIPPING THICK STOCK

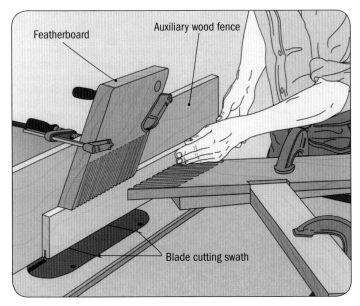

Featherboard
Auxiliary wood fence
Blade cutting swath

Starting the Cut

To resaw a board, position the rip fence for the width of cut and attach
a high auxiliary wood fence. Crank the blade below the table and place
the workpiece over the table insert. To secure the workpiece, clamp one
featherboard to the fence above the blade, and a second featherboard
halfway between the blade and the front of the table. Rest the second
featherboard on a wood scrap so that it supports the middle of the
workpiece; clamp another board at a 90° angle to the featherboard
for extra pressure, as shown. Remove the workpiece and set the
blade height to a maximum of 1½ inches for softwood or 1 inch for
hardwood. To start the cut, feed the workpiece into the blade *(above)*.
Continue cutting at a steady rate until your fingers are about 3 inches
from the blade.

RIPPING THICK STOCK *(continued)*

First Pass

With the saw still running, move to the back of the table. Use one hand to press the workpiece flush against the rip fence *(right)* and the other hand to pull it past the blade. Flip the workpiece over and repeat the cutting procedures in steps 1 and 2.

Completing the Cut

Raise the blade height and make another pass along each edge of the workpiece *(right)*. Make as many passes as necessary, raising the blade height after each pass, until the blade cuts through the workpiece completely.

TAPERS

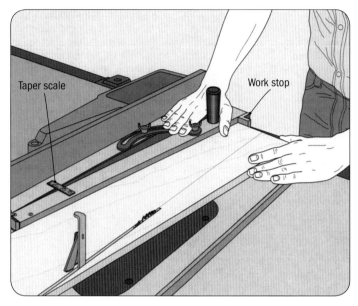

Taper scale

Work stop

Commercial Jig

To cut a workpiece so that one end is narrower than the other, make a taper cut. Hold the jig flush against the rip fence and pivot the hinged arm with the work stop until the taper scale indicates the cutting angle—in degrees or inches per foot. Mark a cutting line on the workpiece, then seat it against the work stop and hinged arm. Position the fence so that the cutting line on the workpiece is aligned with the saw blade. With the jig and workpiece clear of the blade, turn on the saw. Use your left hand to hold the workpiece against the jig and your right hand to slide the jig and workpiece as a unit across the table, feeding the workpiece into the blade *(above)*; ensure neither hand is in line with the blade. Continue cutting at a steady rate until the blade cuts through the workpiece.

(Caution: Saw blade guard removed for clarity.)

TAPERS *(continued)*

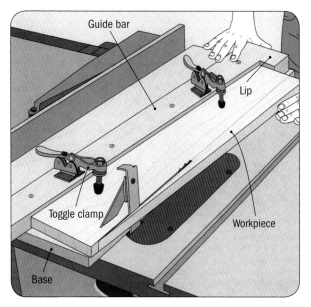

Guide bar

Lip

Toggle clamp

Workpiece

Base

Shopmade Jig

Build a jig exactly like the one shown on page 126 but without the handle. To position the workpiece for the taper cut, raise the saw blade to its highest setting. Butt one side of the jig base against the blade and position the rip fence flush against the other side of the base. Mark a cutting line on the workpiece, then place it on the base, aligning the line with the edge of the taper jig's base nearest the blade. Holding the workpiece securely, position the guide bar against it, with the lip snugly against the end of the workpiece. Screw the guide bar to the base and press the toggle clamps down to secure the workpiece to the jig base. Set the blade height. With the jig and workpiece clear of the blade, turn on the saw. With your left hand pressing the workpiece toward the rip fence, slide the jig and workpiece steadily across the table, making sure that neither hand is in line with the blade *(above)*.

CHAPTER 6

Crosscutting Wood to Length

As cutting with the grain is synonymous with the use of the rip fence, so crosscutting is defined by the device used to make the cut: the miter gauge. The general technique for making a crosscut, begins with correct hand placement to keep the workpiece both flat on the table and firmly against the miter gauge. The workpiece is fed into the blade at a steady rate. As with ripping, make sure scrap pieces do not pile up, and keep both hands out of line with the blade. Keep the rip fence well away from the blade to prevent any cut-off part of the workpiece from becoming trapped between the blade and fence and kicking back.

The slower the feed, the smoother the cut. Although a combination blade can be used for crosscutting, a crosscut blade will produce a finer cut.

With a long workpiece, attach an extension to the miter gauge—normally, a piece of hardwood 3 to 4 inches wide and 2 feet long. Use the miter gauge extension in conjunction with a stop block to make repeat cuts.

For wide panels or long boards, a shop-made crosscutting jig will ensure very accurate cuts. The jig can also be used for smaller pieces. Many experienced woodworkers consider it the single most indispensable accessory for crosscutting.

Making a crosscut

Before measuring or marking a workpiece for a crosscut, cut one end of it square. To avoid jamming the blade, align the workpiece with the blade so that it will trim ½ inch or so. With the thumbs of both hands hooked over the miter gauge, hold the

workpiece firmly against the gauge *(right)* and push them together to feed the workpiece into the blade. **(Caution: Blade guard removed for clarity.)**

Checking for Square

Use a combination square to confirm that the cut end of the workpiece forms a 90° angle with the edge. With the workpiece and square held up to the light, there should be no gap visible. Mark an X on the cut end to help you remember which end has been squared.

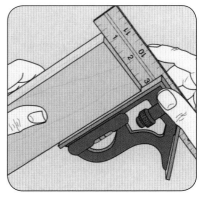

REPEAT CROSSCUTS

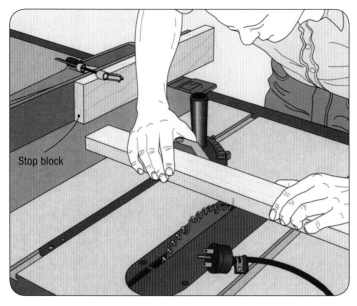

Stop block

Setting Up the cut

Clamp a board to the rip fence as a stop block. To prevent jamming
the workpiece between the stop and the blade—which could lead to
kickback—position the stop far enough toward the front of the table
so that the workpiece will clear the stop before reaching the blade. To
line up the cut, hold the workpiece against the miter gauge and push
the gauge and workpiece forward until the workpiece touches the saw
blade. Slide the workpiece along the miter gauge until the cutting mark
is aligned with the blade (*above*). Be sure to unplug the saw before you
work on this set-up.

REPEAT CROSSCUTS *(continued)*

Positioning the Rip Fence

Holding the workpiece firmly against the miter gauge, pull both back from the blade and butt the stop block against the workpiece *(left)*. Lock the rip fence in position. Check to see that the workpiece does not contact the stop block when the workpiece reaches the blade.

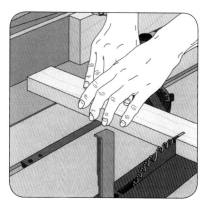

Making the Cut

Set the end of the workpiece flush against the stop block. With the thumbs of both hands hooked over the miter gauge, hold the workpiece firmly against the gauge and push them together to feed the workpiece into the blade *(left)*. **(Caution: Blade guard removed for clarity.)**

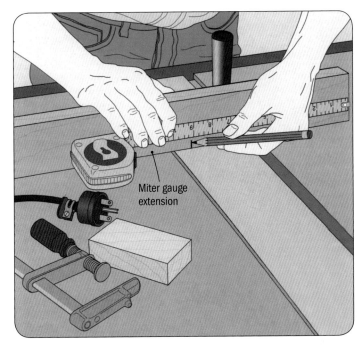

Miter gauge extension

Stop Block

Screw a board to the miter gauge as an extension, ensuring that one end of it extends beyond the saw blade. Push the miter gauge to cut off the end of the extension. Turn off the saw, then slide the miter gauge to the front of the table. Measure and mark the length of cut on the extension *(above)*. Align a wood block with the mark and clamp it in place as a stop block.

REPEAT CROSSCUTS *(continued)*

Stop block

Making the Cut

For each cut, butt the end of the workpiece against the stop block. With the thumbs of both hands hooked over the miter gauge, hold the workpiece firmly against the gauge and push them together, feeding the workpiece into the blade *(above)*. **(Caution: Blade guard removed for clarity.)**

CROSSCUTTING WIDE PANELS

Miter gauge extension

Reversing the Miter Gauge

If a workpiece is wider than the distance between the front edge of the table and the saw blade, the miter gauge cannot be used to begin a crosscut in its usual position—in front of the blade. Instead, remove the gauge and insert it in the miter slot from the back of the table; for extra stability, screw a wooden extension to the gauge. To begin the cut, hold the extension with one hand while pressing the workpiece against it with the other hand. Feed the workpiece steadily into the blade until the trailing end of the workpiece reaches the front of the table.

(Caution: Blade guard removed for clarity.)

CROSSCUTTING WIDE PANELS *(continued)*

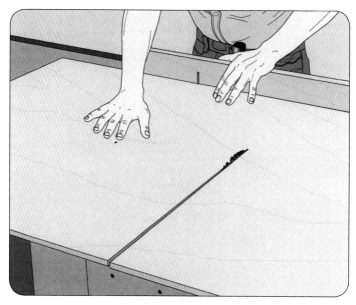

Completing the Cut

Turn off the saw when the blade is far enough through the workpiece to allow the miter gauge to return to its usual position, using a hands-free switch *(page 61)*, if possible, so both hands remain on the workpiece. Insert the miter gauge into its slot from the front of the table and complete the cut, holding the workpiece against the extension *(above)*.

*Shop*Tip

Clamp-On Fence

If your table saw does not have an extension, or you are working with panels that are too large to cut with a miter gauge, you can crosscut these panels by clamping a square 1-by-3 fence to the underside of the panel. Use a 1-by-3 that is longer than the panel is wide and carefully position it underneath perpendicular to the panel's long edge, then clamp the fence to the panel with C clamps. Guide the fence along the outer edge of your saw's table as you make the cut.

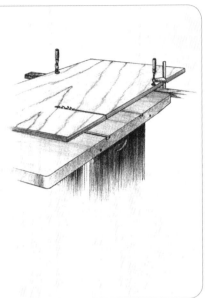

Angles and Bevels

One of the reasons the table saw is so versatile is both the miter gauge and the blade can be angled, producing not only straight cuts but miter, bevel, and compound cuts as well. Miters of between 30° and 90° are cut by angling the miter gauge. Saw blades can be tilted from 45° to 90° *(page 28)*, producing bevel cuts. And by angling both the miter gauge and the saw blade, a one can make a compound cut.

When the blade is tilted, position the miter gauge or rip fence so that the blade angles away from it. This way the workpiece is pushed away from the blade rather than pulled toward it, reducing danger.

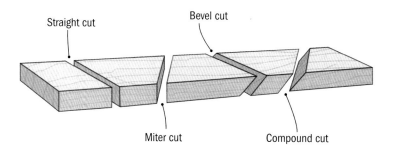

Straight cut

Bevel cut

Miter cut

Compound cut

REPEATED ANGLE CUTS

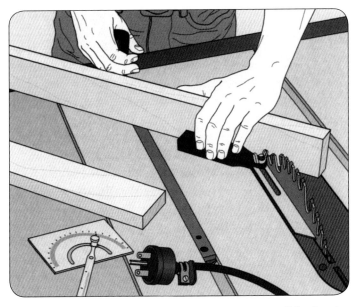

Screw a wooden extension to the miter gauge, then use a sliding bevel to set the desired cutting angle of the gauge *(above)*. If you are making a compound cut, use the sliding bevel to set the blade angle *(page 28)*. Push the miter gauge to cut off the end of the extension. Place the workpiece against the extension and line up the cutting mark with the blade. Clamp a stop to the extension at the opposite end of the workpiece. To make each cut, hold the workpiece firmly against the extension and, keeping both hands out of line with the saw blade, push the workpiece steadily into the blade.

BEVEL RIP

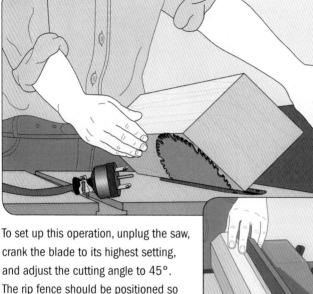

To set up this operation, unplug the saw, crank the blade to its highest setting, and adjust the cutting angle to 45°. The rip fence should be positioned so the blade is tilted away from it. Lay one face of the leg blank on the blade with a corner resting on the saw table, then butt the fence against the stock *(top)* and lock it in place. To make the first cut, butt the stock face-down against

the rip fence a few inches in front of the blade. Adjust the cutting height until one tooth just protrudes beyond the face of the workpiece. Feed the blank into the blade, straddling the fence with your hand. Rotate the leg 90° clockwise and repeat the cut on the adjacent face. Continue in this manner until all the sides are cut.

RAISING A PANEL

End Grain

Cut the panel back to size on this table saw. To determine the blade angle for raising the panel, draw a ¼-inch square at the bottom corner, then mark a line from the front face of the panel through the inside corner of the square to a point on the bottom edge ⅛ inch from the back face (inset). Hold the panel against an auxiliary wood fence and adjust the blade angle until it aligns with the marked line. Adjust the height of the cutting edge until the outside tip of one tooth extends beyond the face of the panel, then clamp a guide block to the workpiece to ride along the top of the fence. Feed the panel into the blade, keeping it flush against the fence while pushing it forward with the guide block (below). Test-fit the cut end in a groove. If less than ¼ inch of the panel enters the groove, move the fence a little closer to the blade and make another pass. Repeat the cut at the other end of the panel.

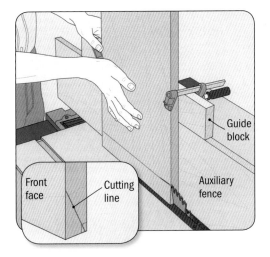

Guide block

Front face

Cutting line

Auxiliary fence

RAISING A PANEL *(continued)*

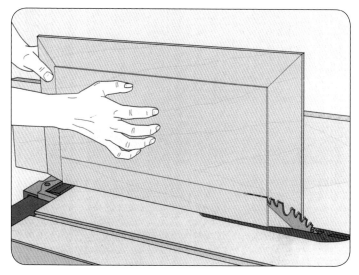

Cutting with the Grain

Set the panel on edge and feed it into the blade, then turn the panel over to cut the remaining edge (above). No guide block is needed for these cuts, but take care to keep the back flush against the fence. Cutting into the end grain of the panel first—beveling the top and bottom before the sides—helps reduce tearout.

Work Supports

Supporting long planks and large panels as they are fed across a saw table ranks as one of the most cumbersome tasks in the woodworking shop. Outfeed tables can be attached to most saws, but they tend to take up a lot of floor space.

Commercial roller stands, like the one shown in the photo below, make better use of shop space; they can also be moved easily to where they are needed and adjusted to height. The shop-made stands described below and on the following page share the advantages of the store-bought variety, with the additional benefit of being easy and inexpensive to build. They can also be dismantled and stored.

A commercial roller stand supports a board being ripped on a radial arm saw. The stand should be set ¼-inch below the level of the saw table and positioned two feet from its edge.

TEMPORARY ROLLER STAND

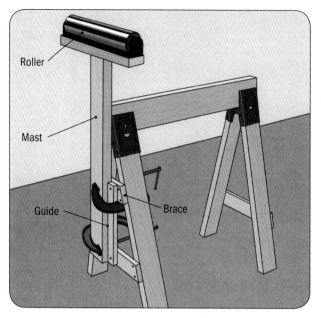

Roller

Mast

Guide

Brace

With only a sawhorse, two C clamps, and a commercial roller, you
can make a simple roller stand like the one shown above. Make
a T-shaped mast for the roller that is long enough to hold it at a
suitable height. Screw the roller to the horizontal part of the mast.
Add a brace to the side of the horse for clamping the mast in place:
Cut a 1-by-4 to span the legs between the sawhorse bracket and
the original brace and screw it to the legs. Cut a 1-by-2 to span the
two braces and screw it in place as a vertical guide for the mast.
To secure the roller stand to the sawhorse, clamp the mast to the
braces, making sure it is flush against the guide.

ADJUSTABLE ROLLER STAND

To build the roller stand shown at right, start by constructing the frame for the roller, cutting the four pieces from 1-by-4 stock. Glue the frame together with butt joints, adding screws to reinforce the connections. Then bore a hole in the middle of each side of the frame for a ¼-inch-diameter carriage bolt. Locate the hole 3 inches from the bottom of the frame. Insert the bolts from the inside of the frame and screw the roller to the top. As well as the commercial roller shown, two variations that permit you to feed the workpiece from any direction are shown below. Cut the remaining pieces of the stand from 1-by-6 stock, referring to the dimensions provided, then rout a ¼-inch-wide slot down the middle of the two uprights; the slot should be about 14 inches long. Screw the crosspiece to the uprights, aligning the top of the piece with the bottom of the slot. Fasten the uprights and rails to the feet. To guide the roller frame, nail 1-by-1 cleats to the uprights about ¼ inch in from the edges. To set up the stand, position the roller frame between the uprights, fitting the carriage bolts into the slots. Slip washers on the bolts and tighten the wing nuts to set the height of the roller.

Types of Rollers

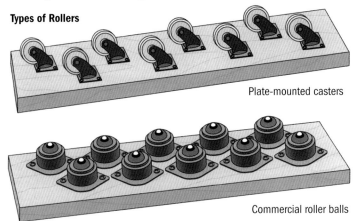

Plate-mounted casters

Commercial roller balls

ADJUSTABLE ROLLER STAND *(continued)*

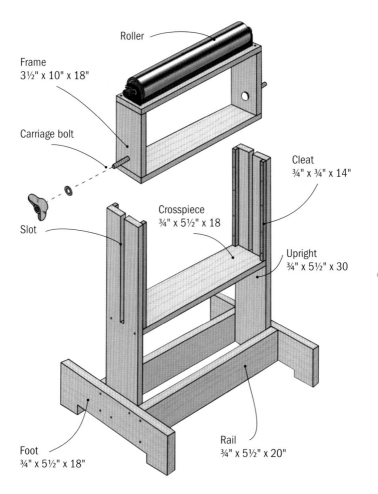

Roller

Frame
3½" x 10" x 18"

Carriage bolt

Slot

Cleat
¾" x ¾" x 14"

Crosspiece
¾" x 5½" x 18

Upright
¾" x 5½" x 30

Foot
¾" x 5½" x 18

Rail
¾" x 5½" x 20"

EXTENSION TABLE

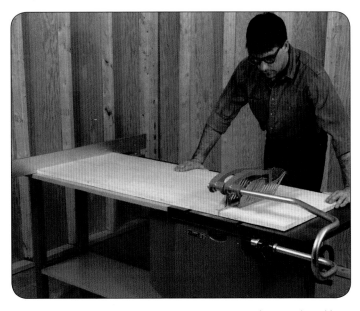

Stationary machines like table saws, come from the manufacturer equipped with tables adequate for most routine operations. But there are some tasks—crosscutting long planks or panels on the table saw for example—that can be awkward or even dangerous to attempt without extending the size of the machine's table. Often, the solution creates a new problem, however, because increasing the size of a stationary machine with a permanent addition can crowd even the roomiest workshop.

An extension table greatly simplifies the task of crosscutting wide panels on the table saw. This commercial model more than doubles the saw table's surface area. It also features a specially designed rip fence that can be moved to any position across the table.

ShopTip

Double-Duty Extension Table

To get maximum use from the work table in your shop, build it so the top is at the same height or slightly lower than the level of your table saw. In addition to being a handy work surface for light jobs, the table can butt against the saw table to serve as an outfeed support. If necessary, modify the table to mate tightly with your saw by cutting a notch in the top to clear the blade guard or other obstructions.

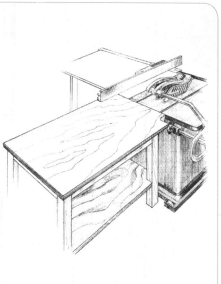

OUTFEED TABLE

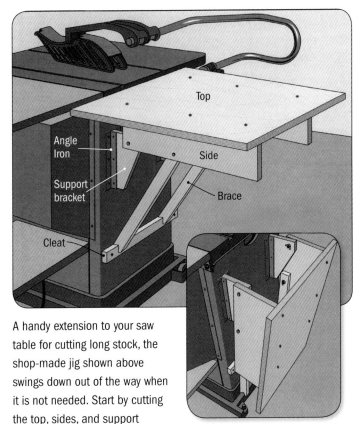

Top

Angle
Iron

Side

Support
bracket

Brace

Cleat

A handy extension to your saw
table for cutting long stock, the
shop-made jig shown above
swings down out of the way when
it is not needed. Start by cutting
the top, sides, and support
brackets from ¾-inch plywood,
sizing the pieces to suit your needs. Then saw the braces
and cleat from 1-by-2 stock, adding an angled notch at
the bottom end of both braces. Screw the sides to the top,
countersinking the fasteners. Next, get ready to attach the jig
to the saw housing. First, attach an angle iron to each side

of both support brackets. Then, have a helper hold the top against the saw table, making sure the two surfaces are level; leave a slight gap between the top and saw table so the jig will fold down without jamming against the table. Now determine the position of the support brackets by butting each against the inside face of a side piece. Mark the holes in the angle irons on the saw housing. Drill a hole for a machine screw at each mark and fasten the angle irons to the housing. Reposition the jig against the saw table and bore holes for a carriage bolt through the sides and support brackets. Use washers under the nuts and bolt heads, and between the sides and brackets. Attach the braces to the sides with bolts spaced about 8 inches from the bracket bolts. Leave all the bolts loose enough for the sides and braces to pivot. Then, holding the jig level again, swing the braces toward the saw housing. Mark the points where the braces contact the housing and screw a cleat to the housing so the cleat's top surface aligns with the two points. To set the jig in position, rest the braces on the cleat. To fold the table down *(inset)*, raise the top slightly, move the braces off the cleat and swing the jig down.

TABLE FOR BENCH-TOP SAW

Added tables steady the work. Shop-built accessory tables
extend the top of this bench-top saw and are adaptable
for use with other machines. For example, a wooden stand
like the one supporting the saw can instead hold a bench
grinder or a jointer at a convenient working height; its short
back legs are fitted with metal casters so the machine on
it can be wheeled to a new location. The extension table
bolted to the left side of the saw can be used with any
power saw to support a sheet of plywood or a long board
held broadside for crosscutting. The freestanding, roller-
topped table behind the saw supports the end of a long
board being cut lengthwise. You can make similar tables for
any size saw. Cabinet shops using large cabinet saws often
surround the machine with auxiliary tables that permit the
easy cutting 4-by-8 sheets of plywood into parts. Some
saws come with sliding table extensions mounted on ball-
bearings, and some woodworkers make their own versions
of these elaborate work supports.

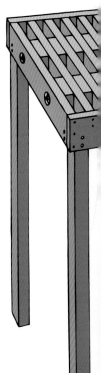

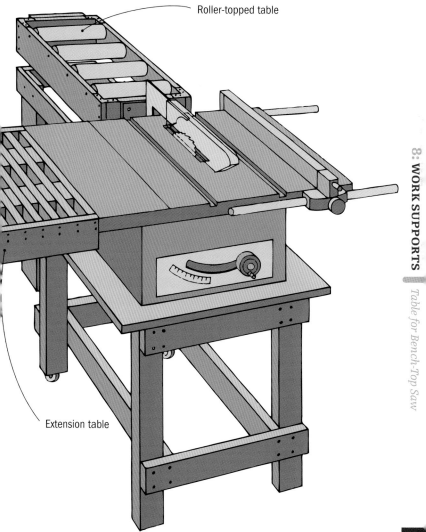

Roller-topped table

Extension table

Hole Locations

For the side rail of an extension table, cut a 1-by-2 rail 1½ inches shorter than the depth of the saw table, front to back. Clamp it to the side of the saw table, centered, top edge

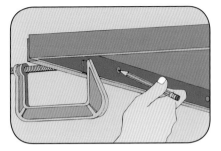

flush with the tabletop. Under the table, find the two holes in the side edge and mark through the holes onto the side rail behind. Unclamp side rail and make counterbored holes at both marks, first drilling the counterbored cavities 1 inch wide and ⅜ inch deep with a 1-inch spade bit. Finish the holes with a ⁵⁄₁₆-inch twist bit.

Drilling

Center a spacer block under one of the side rail holes and line up the edges of the two pieces. Using the ⁵⁄₁₆-inch hole in the side rail as a guide, drill a matching hole through the spacer block. Use the drilled spacer block as a guide for drilling the other blocks. Use the side rail as a guide for drilling ⁵⁄₁₆-inch holes through the other rails and the frame piece, counterboring the 1-by-4 frame piece. Mark the top of each piece after drilling so you can line up the drilled holes later. Hacksaw two ¼-inch beyond than the extension-table width; put a flat washer and a nut on one end of each rod.

For every 1½ inches of width you want the extension table to add, cut one 1-by-2 rail to the same length as the counterbored side rail. For each rail, cut two 4-inch 1-by-2 spacer blocks. Finally, cut one 1-by-4 frame piece to the same length as the rails.

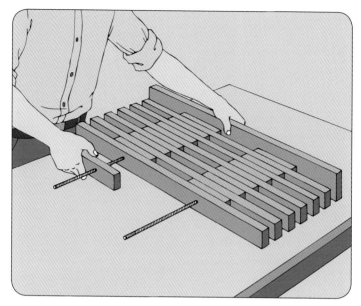

Assembling the Top

Set the top edge of the 1-by-4 frame piece on a flat surface and slide the rods through the holes. Spread a thin coat of wood glue on both sides of two spacer blocks, slide them onto the rods with their top edges down, and press them against the frame piece. Except for the side rail, slide the rest of the pieces onto the rods, alternating rails with pairs of glued spacer blocks. Then slide the side rail onto the rods, with the counterbored side facing out. Put a flat washer and a nut onto the outer ends of both rods, seat them in the counterbored cavities, and tighten the nuts until some of the glue has been squeezed out.

Top edges of rails and spacer blocks should still rest firmly on the flat surface and about 1 inch of threaded rod should extend from the counterbored holes in the inside rail.

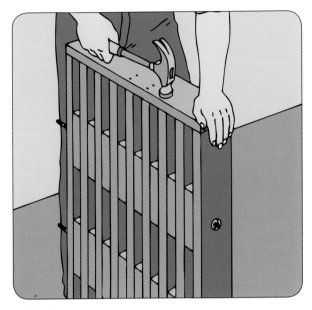

Table Ends

Cut two 1-by-4 frame pieces for the ends, as long as the
width of the extension table. Brush glue onto the rail ends
and fasten the two frame pieces to them with sixpenny
coated box nails, keeping the top edges of the frame flush
with the extension-table top.

Slide the protruding ends of the threaded rods through
the holes in the side of the saw table and prop up the outer
end of the extension table with scrap wood so the tabletop is
level. Cut two 2-by-2 legs 1½ inches shorter than the height
of the tabletop.

TABLE FOR BENCH-TOP SAW *(continued)*

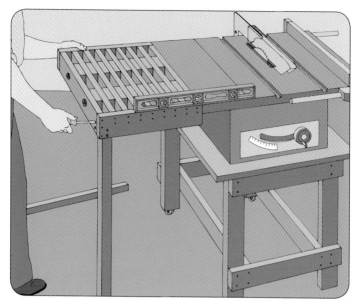

Attach the Legs

Holding a 2-by-2 leg inside one outer corner of the extension table, drill four staggered 3/32-inch pilot holes through the frame pieces and into the leg, and attach the leg with 2-inch wood screws. Attach the other leg in the same way. Under the saw table, thread a lock washer and a nut onto each of the threaded rods and firmly tighten the nuts.

CHAPTER 9

Dados, Rabbets, and Grooves

Several woodworking joints call for channels to be cut into workpieces, allowing boards and panels to fit together tightly and solidly, but inconspicuously.

Four of the most common types of channels are shown on facing page (*top*). They are distinguished from each other by their relationship to the wood grain and their location on a workpiece.

Make the cuts on a table saw with a standard blade by making repeated passes along the workpiece until the entire width of the channel is cut out. A table saw equipped with a dado head can cut a dado, groove, or rabbet much more efficiently.

The wobble dado is a single blade mounted on a hub that can be adjusted to provide varying widths. The greater the tilt—set by a dial on the blade—the wider the channel cut by the blade.

The stacking dado comprises a pair of outside blades that sandwich up to five inside chippers. The width of cut depends on how many chippers are mounted on the saw arbor along with the blades.

Although wobble blades generally are less expensive, stacking dadoes produce more precise widths, flatter bottoms, and cleaner edges with a minimum of tearout.

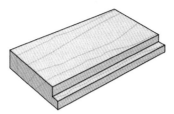

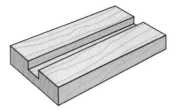

Rabbet: end-to-end cut at edge; either along or against the grain

Groove: end-to-end cut along the grain

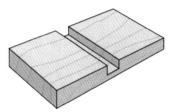

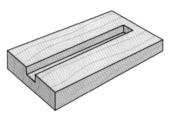

Dado: end-to-end cut across the grain

Stopped groove: cut along the grain that stops short of one or both ends

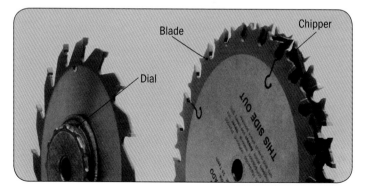

From cutting grooves for shelves in a bookcase to making a rabbet to join two panels together, dado heads are an indispensable and versatile accessory for the table saw.

INSTALLING A DADO HEAD

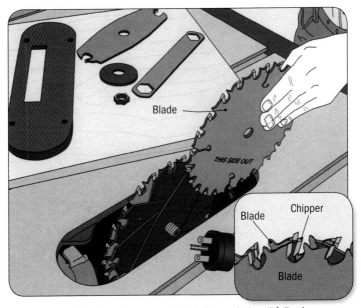

Blade

THIS SIDE OUT

Blade   Chipper

Blade

Remove the blade from the saw and install a dado head following the manufacturer's instructions. For the carbide-tipped stacking dado shown, fit a blade on the arbor with the teeth pointing in the direction of blade rotation. To install a chipper, fit it on the arbor against the blade, with its teeth also pointing in the direction of blade rotation, and centered in gullets between two blade teeth. Fit additional chippers on the arbor the same way, offsetting their teeth from those of the chippers already in place. Then, fit the second blade on the arbor *(top)*, ensuring its teeth do not touch the teeth of the other blade or any chipper resting against it *(inset)*. Install the washer and tighten the nut on the arbor, keeping the blades and chippers in position, again making sure that the teeth of the chippers are not touching any blade teeth. If you cannot tighten the arbor nut all the way, remove the washer. Finally, install a dado table insert on the saw table.

SAWING A DADO

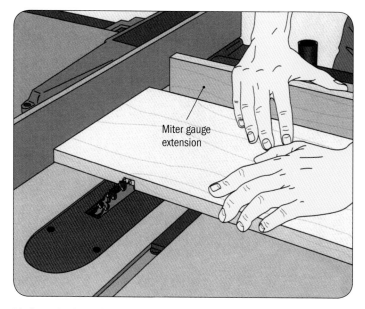

Miter gauge extension

Mark cutting lines for the width of the dado on the leading edge of the workpiece. Butt the cutting lines against the front of the dado head, then position the rip fence flush against the workpiece. Slide the workpiece to the front of the table and set it against the miter gauge— preferably with an extension screwed to it to provide extra stability. To make the cut, slide the miter gauge and the workpiece as a unit into the dado head *(top)*, keeping the workpiece firmly against the fence. (Since the dado head does not cut completely through the workpiece this is one exception to the general rule that the miter gauge and rip fence should never be used at the same time.) Continue feeding the workpiece at a steady rate until the cut is completed.

SAWING A GROOVE

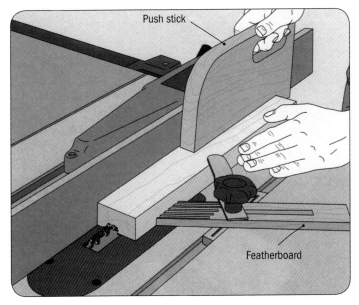

Push stick

Featherboard

Mark cutting lines for the width of the groove on the leading edge of the workpiece. Butt the cutting lines up against the dado head, then position the rip fence flush against the workpiece. For narrow stock, use a featherboard and a push stick to keep your hands away from the dado head. Position your left hand at the front edge of the table to keep the trailing end of the workpiece flush against the fence. Feed the workpiece into the head *(above)* at a steady rate until the cut is completed.

SAWING A RABBET

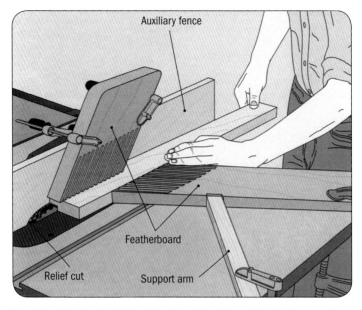

Auxiliary fence

Featherboard

Relief cut

Support arm

Sawing a Rabbet

Install a dado head slightly wider than the rabbet desired, then crank it below the table. Screw a board to the rip fence as an auxiliary fence and mark the depth of the rabbet on it. Position the auxiliary fence directly over the dado head, ensuring that the metal fence is clear of the blade. Turn on the saw and slowly crank up the dado head until it cuts to the marked line, producing a relief cut in the auxiliary fence. Turn off the saw, then mark a cutting line for the inside edge of the rabbet on the workpiece. Butt the cutting line against the dado head, then position the rip fence flush against the workpiece. Clamp two featherboards as shown to hold the workpiece securely against the fence and saw blade; a wooden support arm provides extra stability. Turn on the saw, then feed the workpiece into the dado head *(above)* at a steady rate until the cut is completed; use a push stick, if necessary.

STOPPED GROOVE

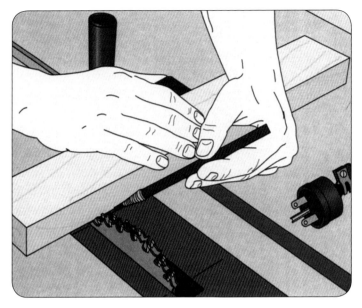

Setting Up

To help you determine the position of the dado head when it is hidden
by the workpiece during this cut, crank the dado head to the depth
of the groove and use a china marker and a straightedge to mark the
points where the head starts and stops cutting *(above)*. Then, mark two
sets of cutting lines on the workpiece: one on its leading end for the
width of the groove; one on its face for the length of the groove. Butt the
cutting lines on the leading end of the workpiece against the front of the
dado head, then position the rip fence flush against the workpiece.

STOPPED GROOVE *(continued)*

Turn on the saw and hold the workpiece just above the dado head, aligning the front cutting line on the workpiece with the dado head cutting mark on the table insert farthest from you. Holding the workpiece tightly against the fence, slowly lower it onto the

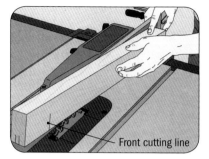

Front cutting line

head *(right)*, keeping both hands clear of the head. When the workpiece sits squarely on the table, feed it forward while pressing it against the fence.

When your left hand comes to within 3 inches of the head, slide your hand along the top edge of the workpiece to the back of the table, hooking your fingers around the table's edge. Continue cutting at a steady rate until the back cutting line on the workpiece aligns with the dado head cutting mark

closest to you. To complete the cut, lift the workpiece off the dado head with your right hand *(right)*, still steadying it against the fence with your left hand hooked around the edge of the table.

Stopped Groove

CHAPTER 10:

Table Saw Joinery

The speed and precision of a table saw make it an obvious choice for cutting joints, particularly repeat cuts. Once a saw is adjusted to cut one box joint or open mortise-and-tenon joint, for example, five or ten more can be cut in short order. The most time-consuming part is the setup; and much depends upon the care taken at this point. A few extra minutes spent at the beginning will result in a strong, long-lasting joint. As always, measure twice and cut once.

Every joint has its own specific qualities and applications. Lap joints are frequently used to make picture frames. Made from two pieces of wood that have half their thickness cut away, a lap joint is simple to make. When glued and clamped, it creates a strong joint that does not require reinforcement.

A box joint, also known as a finger joint, is ideal for carcase work—for making drawers or boxes. It consists of interlocking pins and notches, which are generally one-half or one-quarter the stock's thickness. Once used for mass-produced products such as packing boxes, the box joint creates a strong joint by virtue of the size of the large glue area created by the pins and notches.

The open mortise-and-tenon joint is often found in chairs and desks. Sometimes called a bridle joint, it consists of a projection—or tenon—from one board that slides into a slot—or open mortise—in another board. Like the box joint, it requires a jig, which can be shop-built. The following section describes how to make each of these useful joints.

Lap joint

Box joint

Open mortise-and-tenon joint

LAP JOINT

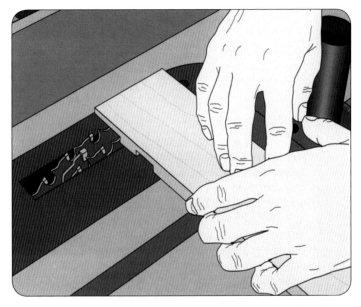

Mark cutting lines for the width of each lap on the leading edge of the workpiece. Butt one cutting line against the outside blade at the front of the dado head, then position the rip fence flush against the workpiece. Slide the workpiece to the front of the table and press it firmly against the fence and the miter gauge. To make the cut, slide the gauge and the workpiece as a unit into the dado head, keeping the workpiece flush against the fence. (This is another exception to the general rule that the miter gauge and rip fence should not be used at the same time.) Continue feeding the workpiece at a steady rate until the cut is made. Make successive passes *(above)*, cutting away the waste until the lap is completed.

BOX JOINT

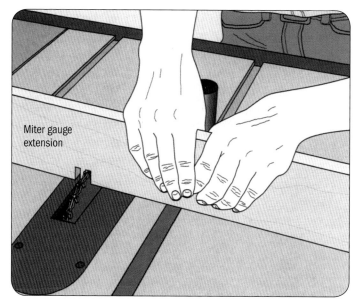

Setting Up the Jig

Cut the notches for a box joint one at a time using a dado head and jig. Clamp a board to the miter gauge as an extension. Crank the dado head to the desired height of the notches and feed the extension into the dado head to create a notch. Position the extension on the miter gauge so that the gap between the notch and the dado head is equal to the notch width, then screw the extension to the gauge. Feed the extension into the dado blade to cut a second notch *(above)*, checking that the gap between the notches equals the notch width. Fit and glue a hardwood key into the notch so that the key projects about an inch from the extension.

BOX JOINT *(continued)*

First Board

Butt one edge of the workpiece against the key, holding it flush against the miter gauge extension. To cut the notch, hook your thumbs around the gauge and slide the workpiece into the dado head *(right)*. Return the workpiece to the front of

the table, fit the notch over the key and repeat the procedure. Continue cutting notches one after another until you reach the opposite edge of the workpiece.

Mating Board

Fit the last notch you cut in the first board over the key, then butt one edge of the mating board against the first board, holding both flush against the miter gauge extension. To cut the first notch in the mating board, slide the two boards across

the table *(right)*, then continue cutting notches in the mating board following the same procedure you used for the first board.

OPEN MORTISE-AND-TENON JOINT

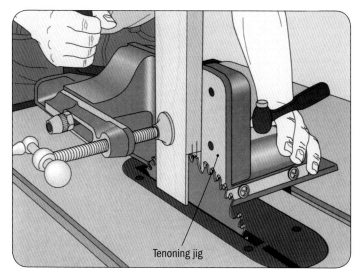

Tenoning jig

Tenon Cheeks

Create a tenon by cutting the cheeks first, and then the shoulders. Install a commercial tenoning jig on the table following the manufacturer's instructions; the model shown slides in the miter slot. Mark cutting lines on the workpiece to outline the tenon, then clamp the workpiece to the jig. Crank the blade to the height of the tenon and position the jig so that one of the tenon cheek cutting lines is butted against the blade. Use the jig handle to slide the jig along the miter gauge slot; loosen the clamp handle to move it sideways. Slide the jig to the front of the table and turn on the saw, then use your right hand to push the jig forward, feeding the workpiece into the blade *(above)*. Continue cutting at a steady rate until the cut is completed. Pull the jig back to the front of the table and turn off the saw. Turn the workpiece around so that the remaining cutting line for the thickness of the tenon is butted against the blade. Cut along it the same way as you made the first cut.

OPEN MORTISE-AND-TENON *(continued)*

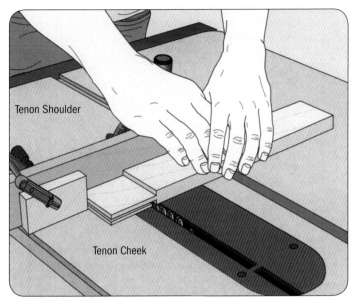

Tenon Shoulders

Screw a board to the miter gauge as an extension. Then crank the blade
to a height equal to the depth of the tenon against the extension, align
one of the tenon shoulder cutting lines against the blade, then butt a stop
block against the workpiece and clamp it in position. Slide the workpiece
to the front of the table and turn on the saw. Hook your thumbs around the
miter gauge to feed the workpiece into the blade and make the cut. Use
a push stick to clear the waste piece off the table. Flip over the workpiece
and butt it against the stop block, then cut the second shoulder *(above)*.

Open Mortise-and-Tenon   **10: TABLE SAW JOINERY**

Within the image: Tenon Shoulder, Tenon Cheek

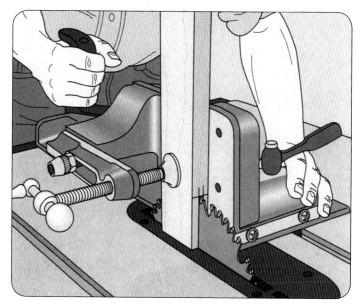

Cutting the Mortise

Reinstall the tenoning jig on the table. Mark cutting lines on the workpiece to outline the mortise, then clamp the workpiece to the jig. Crank the blade to the depth of the mortise and position the jig so that one of the cutting lines is butted against the blade. Slide the jig to the front of the table, then turn on the saw and feed the workpiece into the blade. Pull the jig back and turn off the saw. Turn the workpiece over so that the remaining cutting line is butted against the blade and cut along it *(above)*. Make as many passes as necessary to remove waste between the two cuts. Test-fit the joint and deepen or widen the mortise, if necessary.

Moldings

A table saw is more than just a machine to cut wood. With the proper setup, a saw blade can serve as a milling device to cut cove moldings *(page 120)*. And by replacing the saw blade with a molding head and different sets of cutters, a plain board can become an elaborate molding. The results range from crown moldings for a cabinet to decorative door and frame moldings at a fraction of the cost of store-bought counterparts.

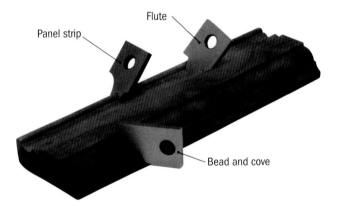

Flute

Panel strip

Bead and cove

Three sets of cutters were used in combination to transform a piece of walnut into an elaborate baseboard molding (left). More than 30 blade profiles are available; by using different cutters or knives—a limitless range of designs can be made.

MOLDING KNIVES

Common Cutter Profiles

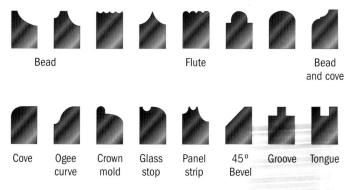

Bead   Flute   Bead and cove

Cove   Ogee curve   Crown mold   Glass stop   Panel strip   45° Bevel   Groove   Tongue

Molding cutters are sold in sets of three, which are installed in a molding head and then fastened onto the arbor. By passing the wood over the cutters repeatedly and raising the molding head slightly each time, a pattern is cut into the wood. The more passes, the deeper the inscription.

Like a dado head, a molding head requires its own table insert with a wide opening to accommodate the width of the cutters. A woodworker can make an insert for each set of cutters by placing a blank piece of wood in the table insert slot and slowly cranking up the molding head—much like making special inserts for saw blades.

Molding heads have a reputation for being dangerous. A few points to keep in mind: Do not cut moldings on short lengths of wood; a piece should be at least 24 inches long. Also, do not cut moldings on narrow strips. Cut the moldings on pieces at least 4 inches wide and then rip to width.

MOLDING HEAD

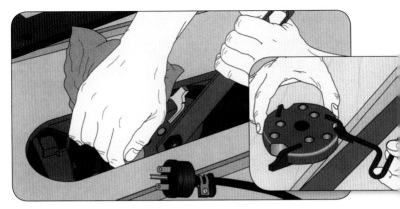

Fit each of the three cutters partway into its slot in the molding head, ensuring that the cutter's beveled edge faces away from the setscrew hole. Install the setscrews into their holes, then use a hex wrench to tighten each screw until the cutters are seated firmly in their slots *(inset)*. Install the molding head on the saw with the flat side of each cutter facing the direction of blade rotation. Grip the molding head with a rag to protect your hand and tighten the arbor nut counterclockwise using a wrench *(above, large)*. A washer is not necessary; the molding head is rigid enough without reinforcement. After the molding head is secured, install a molding-head table insert on the saw table. Rotate the molding head by hand to make sure that the cutters are true and that the unit does not rub against the insert.

Be certain to unplug the saw before working on the molding head.

MAKING FIRST PASSES

Before cutting a molding, screw a board to the rip fence as an auxiliary fence. Position the auxiliary fence directly over the molding head, ensuring that the metal fence is clear of the cutters. Turn on the saw and crank up the molding head gradually to cut a notch in the auxiliary fence to allow for clearance of the cutters. Turn off the saw, then line up the cutting line on the end of the workpiece with the cutters and butt the rip fence against the workpiece. Crank the molding head to its lowest setting. To secure the workpiece, clamp one featherboard to the fence above the saw blade, and a second featherboard to the saw table. Clamp a support board at a 90° angle to the second featherboard, as shown. Remove the workpiece and crank the cutters to ⅛ inch above the table; do not make a full-depth cut in one pass. Turn on the saw and use your right hand to slowly feed the workpiece toward the molding head; use your left hand to keep the workpiece against the rip fence. Finish the cut with a push stick. For a deeper cut, make as many passes as necessary *(above)*, raising the molding head ⅛ inch at a time.

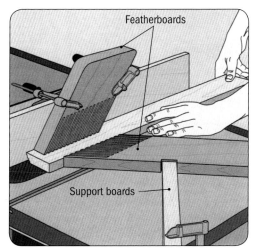

Featherboards

Support boards

MAKING THE FINAL PASS

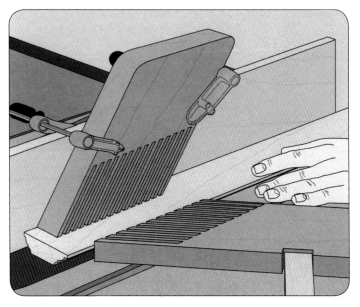

After successive passes have produced the depth of cut desired, crank the molding head up very slightly and pass the workpiece through a final time at half the speed of previous passes *(above)*. By feeding the workpiece slowly, the final cut produces a smooth finish that requires minimal sanding.

SEPARATING THE MOLDING

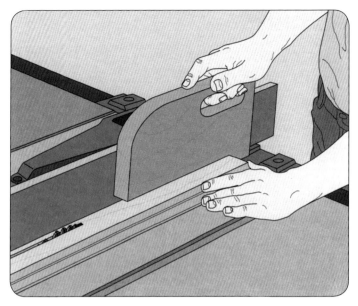

After the proper profile has been cut, separate the molding from the workpiece. Remove the molding head from the arbor and install a rip or combination blade. Feed the board through the blade, using a push stick to keep the workpiece firmly on the table *(above)*; use your left hand or a featherboard to press it flush against the rip fence.

COVE MOLDING

Setting the Width

Build a cove cutting guide in the shape of a parallelogram by fastening two 18-inch-long 1-by-2s to two 9-inch-long 1-by-2s with wing nuts,

forming two sets of parallel arms. Adjust the guide so the distance between the inside edges of the two long arms is the same as the desired width of the cove molding. Then crank up the blade to the maximum depth of the

Cove cutting guide

cove. Lay the guide diagonally across the blade insert and rotate it until the blade, turned by hand, just touches both long arms of the guide *(above)*.

Marking

Using a pencil or china marker, trace guidelines on the table insert and saw table along the inside edges of the long arms of the guide *(right)*. Then outline the desired profile of the cove on the leading end of the

workpiece. Remove the guide, crank the blade to its lowest setting and place the workpiece on the saw table, aligning the marked outline on the workpiece with the guidelines on the saw table.

COVE MOLDING *(continued)*

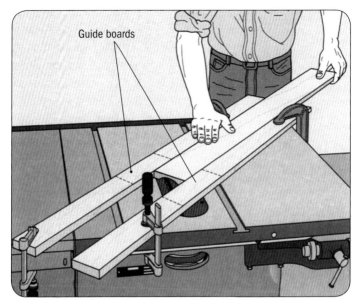

Guide boards

Cutting the Cove

Butt a guide board against each edge of the workpiece; use boards long enough to clamp on opposite sides of the table. Crank the blade ⅛ inch above the table. To make the first pass, feed the workpiece steadily toward the blade with your left hand, while holding the workpiece against the table with your right hand. Finish the cut using a push block. Make as many passes as necessary *(above)*, raising the blade ⅛ inch at a time. For a deep cove, tack a backup board to the top of the workpiece to prevent it from splitting. For a smooth finish that requires little sanding, raise the blade slightly for a last pass and feed the workpiece slowly into it.

Table Saw Jigs

From the time you cut rough lumber to length at the start of a project or miter trim to finish it, your table saw is likely to be your most-used tool. Although many cutting tasks can be accomplished without them, the jigs shown in this chapter will make these operations easier—particularly when the same cut must be repeated on several workpieces.

With its intersecting arms, a table saw miter jig *(page 131)* guarantees miter joints that form perfect 90° angles. The tenoning jigs shown on pages 136 and 137 allow you to cut both parts of open mortise-and-tenon joints on the table saw.

In tandem with your table saw, the raised panel jig *(page 132)* can produce beveled panels for frames.

These jigs will save you time in the shop. An added benefit is that most can be built from scrap wood, making them considerably less costly than store-bought counterparts.

CUTTING JIGS

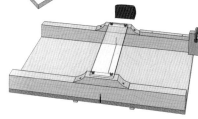

Board-straightening jig
(page 125)
Used on the table saw to true the edges of uneven stock; features a bar that runs in miter slot.

Table saw taper jig
(page 126-127)
For cutting tapers on the table saw, guide bar with toggle clamps is screwed in place to hold workpiece at proper taper angle.

Table saw crosscut jig
(page 128-130)
Adjustable jig used to make crosscuts on the table saw in wide, long, or heavy stock.

Table saw miter jig (page 131)
Similar to the crosscut jig, except with angled arms used to make mating 45° miter cuts.

Cutting Jigs

CUTTING JIGS *(continued)*

Panel-raising jig (page 132-133)
Attaches to the table saw rip fence to bevel the edges of raised panels for frame-and-panel assemblies.

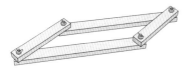

Cove-cutting jig (page 134-135)
Used to set up guide boards on saw table for cutting cove molding.

Tenoning jig (page 136-137)
For cutting both parts of open mortise-and-tenon joints on the table saw; runs along rip fence.

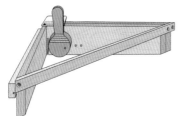

Adjustable tenoning jig (page 138-140)
Used to cut open mortise-and-tenons on the table saw; adjusts to stock of varying thickness.

BOARD-STRAIGHTENING JIG

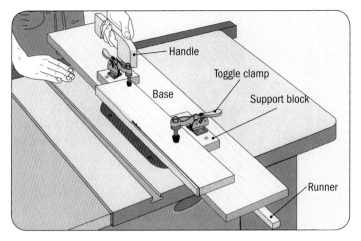

To true uneven boards on a table saw, build the board straightening jig shown above. Built from ¾-inch plywood, the jig slides in the table saw's miter gauge slot, while the board to be straightened is held in place by support blocks and toggle clamps. First cut the base from ¾-inch plywood; make it about 9 inches wide and longer than the width of your saw table. Cut a runner to fit the left-hand miter gauge slot; make it longer than the jig base and position it on the underside of the base so that the inside edge of the base overlaps the blade by ⅛ inch. Screw the runner to the bottom of the jig, countersinking all the screws. Next, screw two support blocks to the base and install toggle clamps on them; position the support blocks so the workpiece is centered on the base. Finally, fashion a handle and attach it to the end of the jig. To use the jig, first trim the inside edge square by running it across the blade, then clamp the board to be straightened to the jig and repeat to true its edges (above).

TAPER JIG

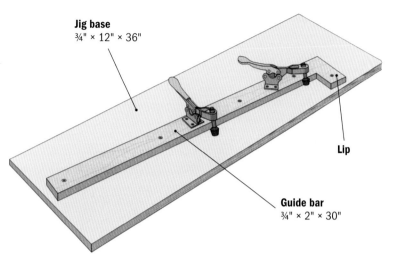

Jig base
¾" × 12" × 36"

Lip

Guide bar
¾" × 2" × 30"

For accurate taper cuts on the table saw, build this jig *(above)* from
¾-inch plywood. Refer to the illustration for suggested dimensions. To
assemble the jig, set the saw blade to its maximum cutting height, butt
one side of the jig base against the blade and position the rip fence
flush against the other side of the base.

TAPER JIG *(continued)*

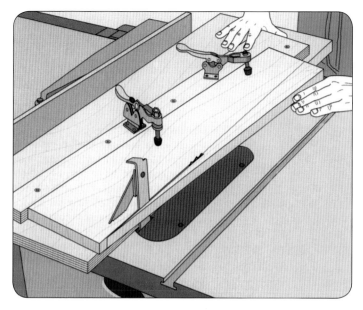

Lower the blade and mark a cutting line for the taper on the workpiece, then set it on the base, aligning the line with the edge of the jig base nearest the blade. Holding the workpiece securely, position the guide bar against it, with the lip snugly against the end of the workpiece. Screw the guide bar to the base and press the toggle clamps down to secure the workpiece to the jig. To make the cut, set the blade height and slide the jig and workpiece across the table, making sure that neither hand is in line with the blade *(above)*:

CROSSCUT JIG

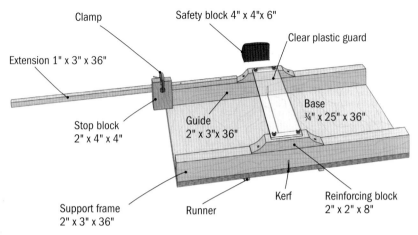

Clamp

Safety block 4" x 4"x 6"

Clear plastic guard

Extension 1" x 3" x 36"

Base ¾" x 25" x 36"

Stop block 2" x 4" x 4"

Guide 2" x 3"x 36"

Support frame 2" x 3" x 36"

Runner

Kerf

Reinforcing block 2" x 2" x 8"

Attaching the Runners

A crosscut jig custom-made for your table saw like the one shown above is especially valuable if you are working with unwieldy stock. Refer to the illustration for suggested dimensions. Start by cutting two 25-inch-long hardwood runners to fit your miter slots. Bore and countersink clearance holes for screws into the undersides of the runners, 3 inches from each end. Place the runners in the slots and slide them out to overhang the back end of the table by about 8 inches. Position the jig base squarely on the wood strips, its edge flush with their overhanging ends, and screw the runners to the base (right). Slide the runners and the base off the front end of the table and drive in the other two screws.

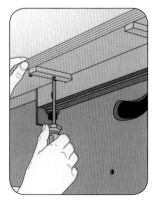

CROSSCUT JIG *(continued)*

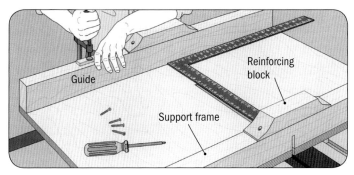

Guide

Reinforcing block

Support frame

Installing the Fence

With the runners still in the miter slots, attach the support frame along the back edge of the jig and glue on the reinforcing block, centered between the runners. Then make a cut through the support frame and three-quarters of the way across the base. Turn off the saw and lower the blade. Screw a reinforcing block to the guide and position the guide along the front edge of the jig, using a carpenter's square to ensure that it is square with the saw kerf. Clamp the guide in place *(above)* and screw it to the base from underneath the jig, making sure you countersink the fasteners. Glue the safety block to the outside face of the guide, again centered on the kerf. Raise the saw blade and finish the cut, sawing completely through the guide but only slightly into the safety block. Mount a clear plastic sheet over the saw kerf as a blade guard, fastening it to the reinforcing blocks with wing nuts or screws.

12: TABLE SAW JIGS

Crosscut Jig

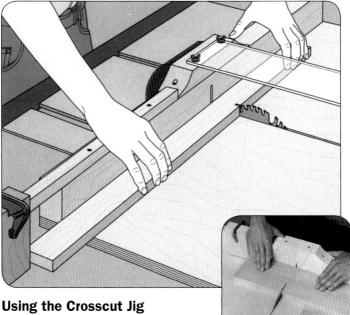

Using the Crosscut Jig

For making repeat cuts to the same length, screw an extension to the right side of the guide and clamp a stop block to it. Cut a notch in the block to hold the clamp in place when it is loosened. To use the jig, fit the runners into the miter slots and slide

the jig toward the back of the table until the blade enters the kerf. Hold the workpiece against the guide, slide the stop block to the desired position, and clamp it in place. With the workpiece held firmly against the guide and the stop block, slide the jig steadily across the table *(inset)*, feeding the workpiece into the blade.

MITER JIG

Miter arm

Stop block

Build a crosscut jig without an extension or a safety block. Then, cut two 12-inch-long 1-by-4s and place them at 90° to each other in the middle of the jig, centered on its kerf. Turn the jig over and screw the 1-by-4s to the jig. To make a series of cuts, butt the workpiece against the left arm of the jig, align the cutting line on the workpiece with the saw blade and clamp a stop block to the arm at the end of the workpiece. Cut through the workpiece, holding it firmly against the arm and stop block *(above)*. Cut the mating piece of the joint the same way on the right arm of the jig. Use the stop blocks as guides for additional cuts to the same length.

The table saw miter jig is similar to the crosscut jig except that instead of an extension and safety block it features two 12-inch-long 1-by-4 miter arms. Placed at 90° to each other in the middle of the jig, the arms ensure a workpiece mitered along one guide will form a perfect 90° corner with a board cut along the other arm.

Miter Jig

PANEL-RAISING JIG

Making the Jig

To raise a panel on the table saw without adjusting the blade angle, use the shopmade jig shown at right. Refer to the illustration for suggested dimensions. Screw the lip along the bottom edge of the angled fence, making sure to position the screws where they will not interfere with the blade. Prop the angled fence against the auxiliary fence at the same angle as the cutting line marked out on the panel to be raised. Use a sliding bevel to transfer this angle to triangular-shaped supports that will fit between the two fences and cut the supports to fit. Fix the supports in place with screws *(below)*.

Angled fence
12" x 30"

Lip
1¼" x 30"

Auxiliary
fence
9" x 30"

Support

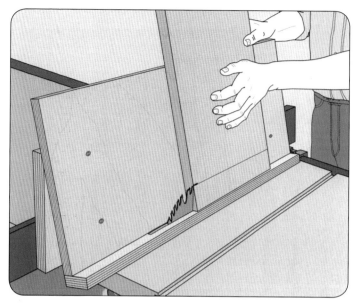

Raising a Panel

Shift the rip fence to position the jig on the saw table with the joint of the lip and angled fence over the blade; ensure that the screws are well clear of the table opening. Turn on the saw and crank the blade up slowly to cut a kerf through the lip. Next, seat the panel in the jig and adjust the height of the blade until a single tooth is protruding beyond the front of the panel. Make a test cut in a scrap board the same thickness as the panel and then test its fit in the frame groove. Adjust the position of the fence or blade, if necessary, and cut the actual panel, beveling the end grain first *(above)*.

COVE-CUTTING JIG

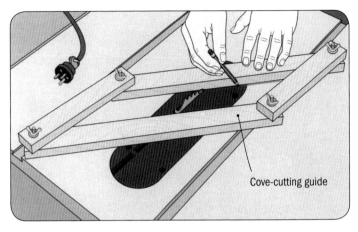

Cove-cutting guide

Making the Jig

Fashion molding on the table saw with the help of the cove-cutting guide shown above. To construct the jig, fasten two 18-inch-long 1-by-2s to two 9-inch-long 1-by-2s with carriage bolts and wing nuts, forming two sets of parallel arms. Adjust the jig so the distance between the inside edges of the two long arms equals the width of the cove. Crank the blade to the desired depth of cut. Lay the guide across the blade and rotate it until the blade, turned by hand, just touches the inside edges of the arms. Then run a pencil along the inside edges of the long arms to trace guidelines across the table insert *(above)*.

COVE-CUTTING JIG *(continued)*

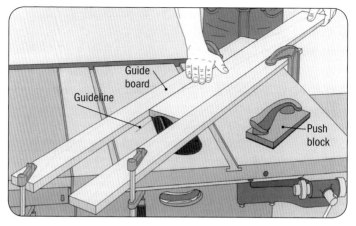

Guide board

Guideline

Push block

Sawing a Cove

Remove the guide and lower the blade beneath the table. Outline the desired cove profile on the leading end of the workpiece, then set the stock on the saw table, aligning the marked outline with the guidelines on the table insert. Butt guide boards against the edges of the workpiece and clamp them parallel to the guidelines; use boards long enough to span the saw table. Crank the blade ⅛ inch above the table. To make the first pass, feed the workpiece steadily *(above)*, using push blocks when your hands approach the blade area. Make as many passes as necessary, raising the blade ⅛ inch at a time.

Cove-Cutting Jig

TENONING JIG

Making the Jig

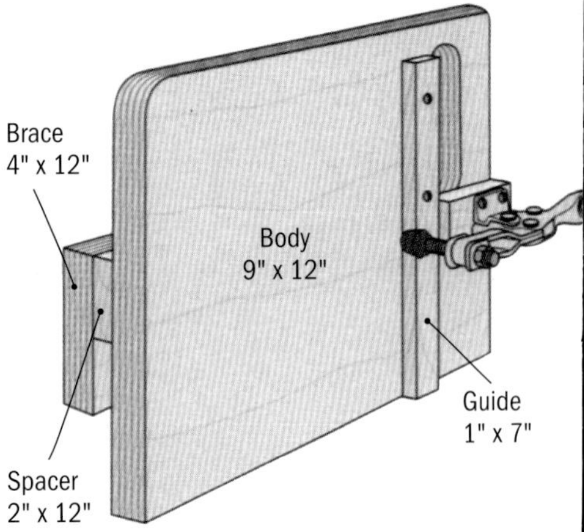
Brace
4" x 12"
Body
9" x 12"
Guide
1" x 7"
Spacer
2" x 12"

Easy to assemble, the fence-straddling jig shown at right works well for cutting two-shouldered open mortise-and-tenon joints. Refer to the dimensions suggested in the illustration, making sure the thickness of the spacer and width of the brace allow the jig to slide smoothly along your rip fence without wobbling. Cut the body and brace from ¾-inch plywood and the guide and spacer from solid wood. Saw an oval hole for a handle in one corner of the jig body and attach the guide to the body directly in front of the handle hole, making sure that the guide is perfectly vertical. (The blade may notch the bottom of the guide the first time you use the jig.) Screw a small wood block to the body below the handle and attach a toggle clamp to the block. Finally, fasten the spacer and brace in place.

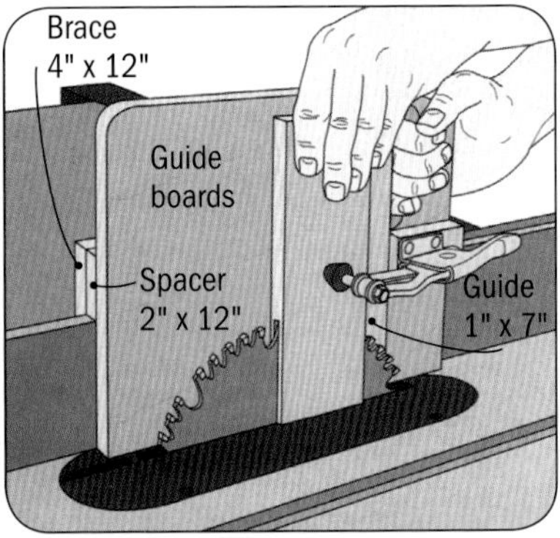
Brace
4" x 12"
Guide
boards
Spacer
2" x 12"
Guide
1" x 7"

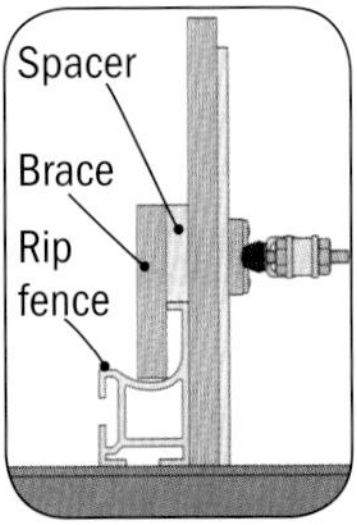
Spacer
Brace
Rip
fence

TENONING JIG *(continued)*

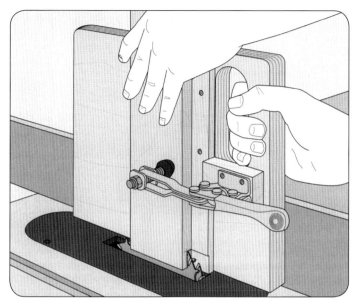

Sawing the Joint

Place the jig astride the fence. Butt the workpiece against the jig guide and clamp it in place. Position the fence to align the cutting marks on the board with the blade and slide the jig along the fence to make the cut *(above)*.

Tenoning jig

ADJUSTABLE TENONING JIG

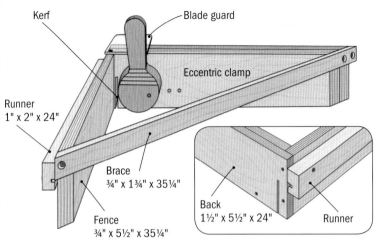

Kerf

Blade guard

Eccentric clamp

Runner
1" x 2" x 24"

Brace
¾" x 1¾" x 35¼"

Back
1½" x 5½" x 24"

Runner

Fence
¾" x 5½" x 35¼"

Assembling the Jig

The jig shown above can be used on the table saw to cut both parts of
an open mortise-and-tenon joint. Refer to the illustration for suggested
dimensions. Cut the jig fence and back from three pieces of ¾-inch
plywood and saw a 45° bevel at one end of each board; the pieces
should be wider than the height of your saw's rip fence. Fasten two
pieces together face-to-face to fashion the back, then use countersunk
screws to attach the fence and back together in an L shape; make
sure the fasteners will not be in the blade's path when you use the jig
(above, inset). Next, cut the brace from solid stock, bevel its ends and
attach it along the top edges of the fence and back, forming a triangle.
Cut the runner from solid wood and attach it to the fence so that the
jig runs smoothly across the table without wobbling. The runner in this
illustration has been notched to fit the particular design of the saw's rip
fence. Finally, cut a piece of clear plastic as a blade guard and screw it
to the jig back flush with its front face.

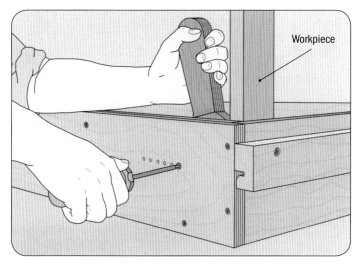

Eccentric Clamp

Make the clamp by face-gluing three pieces of ¾-inch plywood and cutting the assembly into the shape shown. Bore a pilot hole through the jig back and the clamp, then fasten the clamp in place; wedge one of your workpieces between the edge of the clamp and the fence as you drive the screw. Offset the fastener so the clamp can pivot eccentrically *(above)*. Drill additional holes in the jig back to enable you to move the clamp to accommodate stock of varying thicknesses.

ADJUSTABLE TENONING JIG *(continued)*

Pivot point

Cutting a Tenon

Set the jig on the saw table in front of the blade with the runner and fence straddling the rip fence. Secure the workpiece in the jig by turning the eccentric clamp, and position the rip fence so that the blade is in line with a tenon cheek cutting mark on the workpiece. Feed the jig into the blade. Your first use of the jig will produce a kerf in the back. Flip the workpiece in the jig and repeat to cut the other cheek *(above)*. Remove the jig from the table, lower the cutting height to the level of the shoulders, and shift the rip fence to cut the tenon shoulders.

Adjustable Tenoning Jig   **12: TABLE SAW JIGS**

Miter-Gauge Angle-Setting Jig

To keep track of non-standard angles that you commonly use on your table saw's miter gauge, make a set of angle-setting jigs. Simply cut two 1-by-2s and clamp them to the miter gauge, one against the bar and one against the face. Screw them together into an angled L shape and mark down the angle they form on the jig. Use the device like a sliding bevel to set the miter gauge quickly to a specific angle.

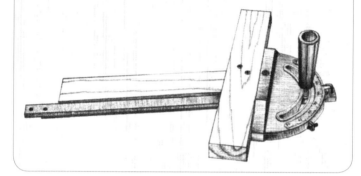

Index

INDEX

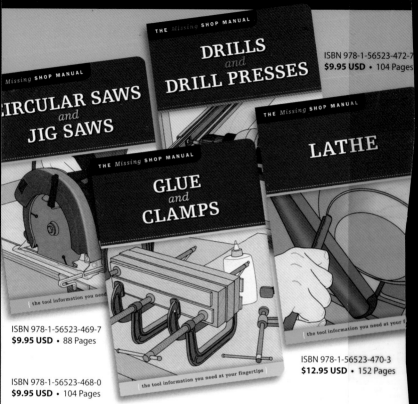